North Wales Classics

Tremadog
Cwm Silyn
Cloggy
Llanberis
Lliwedd
Ogwen
Carneddau
Betws y Coed
Welsh Winter

Additional text by Alan James,
Chris Craggs and Stephen Horne

Printed by John Browns, Nottingham
Distributed by Cordee (www.cordee.co.uk)
All maps by ROCKFAX.

Published by ROCKFAX April 2010
© UKClimbing Limited 2010

www.rockfax.com
www.ukclimbing.com

All Rockfax books are printed in the UK.
We only use paper made from wood fibre from
sustainable forests and produced according to ISO
14001 environmental management standard.

ISBN 978-1-873341-17-9

Cover: Sarah Burmester on *One Step in the
Clouds* (VS) - *page 37* - at Tremadog.
Photo: Jack Geldard

This Page: Martin Chester on *Cemetery
Gates* (E1) - *page 93* - on Dinas Cromlech.
Photo: Mark Reeves

Tremadog

Cwm Silyn

Cloggy

Llanberis

Lliwedd

Ogwen

Carneddau

Betws y Coed

Welsh Winter

North Wales has one of the most concentrated selections of adventurous climbing in the whole of Europe. Almost every valley is flanked by walls of superb quality and well-featured rock giving a lifetime's worth of routes at all grades and all within an hour radius.

From the mountain-magnificence of Cloggy, to the sun-kissed single pitch routes on the Upper Tier of Tremadog, North Wales can cater for almost every climber's need. Many of the routes documented in this book are historically significant; major milestones in British rock climbing. The cliffs of North Wales have long called out to climbers, and that magical attraction hasn't waned.

The Llanberis Pass is perhaps the most famous rock climbing valley in Britain, and for good reason. The routes there are fantastic, generally easy to access and have picturesque views. Its bigger sister; the Ogwen valley, is a low-grade paradise with many easier-angled cliffs that offer good protection and ample belay stances with a wild and commanding outlook across to the Carneddau.

But it isn't all Llanberis and Ogwen. In this book you will find a spread of routes, at a variety of grades at the best venues, but we have also picked a few cliffs that you might not have heard of. Some low-lying outcrops such as Clogwyn y Cyrau might not rival the Idwal Slabs for long mountain routes, but they offer another weather option, are close to the popular village of Betws y Coed, and could be just the ticket for a couple of hours of fun on the way back down the A5.

We have worked hard to keep the guide in a pocket-sized format, crow-baring in as much info as possible, making the photographs full page in size and crystal clear. North Wales Classics is the Tardis of the climbing world and it contains all the info you need in a size that is useful, meaning it won't weigh you down on that balancy crux.

Mick Ryan on *Pinnacle Rib Route* (VDiff) - *page 123* - East Face of Tryfan. Photo: Alan James

Introduction 2

Welsh Winter. 4
Mountain Rescue, Access . . 6
Topo and Symbol Key. 8
Gear 10
Grades 12
Shops, Walls and Guides . . 14
Pubs and Shops 14
Acknowledgements. 16

Tremadog 18
Cwm Silyn 48
Clogwyn Du'r Arddu 54
Llanberis Pass North 72
Llanberis Pass South 94
Lliwedd 108
Ogwen 116
Carneddau 152
Betws y Coed 168
Welsh Winter 178

Route Index 204
General Index and Map . . . 208
Advertiser Index 208

A climber commits to the tricky move that gives access to the upper groove of *Shadrach* (VS) - *page 41* - Bwlch y Moch at Tremadog. Photo: Jack Geldard

Tremadog

Cwm Silyn

Cloggy

Llanberis

Lliwedd

Ogwen

Carneddau

Betws y Coed

Welsh Winter

3

Winter climbing in Wales has suffered in recent years. Not from a lack of ice, but from a lack of information. Not any more. This winter section covers the best and most reliable venues including the classic gullies of the Trinity Face and the rarely-formed but absolutely essential ice climbs of Cascade and Central Icefall Direct in the Llanberis Pass.

Situated geographically close-together are the major ice lines of Cwm Idwal and the modern mixed climbs of Clogwyn Du. This particular section of the Glyderau offers a range of winter styles and grades, from perfect ice gullies to desperate cutting-edge mixed challenges. Are your crampons sharp?

Not all of Wales' winter routes are short and easy to access. The huge cliff of The Black Ladders rivals anything in Scotland and is home to long and committing adventures that give a full and tiring day out. The routes on this white citadel are utterly brilliant.

Photographed here in full colour and full winter garb, the routes can be seen for what they are; simply unmissable.

Grades

All climbing grades are subjective and none more so than winter grades. With the highly fickle conditions found in Wales, the routes can be much harder than their grade. Thaw conditions, dangerously thin ice, unconsolidated snow, it is all out there. Be prepared for a tough time, but if you do find a route that is in perfect condition and feels easy for the grade, don't complain - take the tick!

Grade Definitions
More on - www.mcofs.org.uk

I	Simple snow slopes with possible corniced exits.
II	Gullies with high-angled snow and corniced exits. Easy buttress routes.
III	Gullies with steeper ice or mixed sections. Moderate buttress climbs.
IV	Steep gullies or near-vertical icefalls. Technical buttress routes.
V	Vertical ice. Steep and technical buttress routes.
VI	Long sustained vertical ice routes. Vertical and technical buttress routes.
VII	Thin vertical ice routes, fragile ice. Very steep and technical buttresses.
VIII	Very serious overhanging ice. Sustained, steep, technical buttresses.
IX	Extremely technical and sustained routes on buttresses.

Technical Grades - The technical grade is usually the same numerical value as the main grade. A higher technical grade indicates a route with a short technical section only, a lower technical grade indicates a route with easier climbing but poor belays and protection.

Tremadog

Cwm Silyn

Cloggy

Llanberis

Lliwedd

Ogwen

Carneddau

Betws y Coed

Welsh Winter

Jon Ratcliffe on the first pitch of *The Devil's Appendix* (VI) - *page 194* - in Cwm Idwal. Photo: Jack Geldard

Mountain Rescue

In the event of an accident requiring the assistance of Mountain Rescue:
Dial 999 and ask for 'POLICE - MOUNTAIN RESCUE'
North Wales Mountain Rescue Association - www.nwmra.org

Access

None of the crags in this guidebook have major access problems, and all that is required to ensure continued freedom of access is a responsible approach. Otherwise the freedoms already won could be so easily lost. This includes making sure that your car is parked sensibly, that you don't climb over fences or walls, and that you stick to footpaths where possible. If you do encounter access problems, contact the **BMC**
The British Mountaineering Council, 177-179 Burton Road,
West Didsbury, Manchester, M20 2BB - **www.thebmc.co.uk**

Guidebooks

The Climbers' Club has published a number of guides to areas in North Wales which give full coverage of all the routes on the crags in this book, plus many more crags as well. If you enoyed the routes in this book then take a look at the following books:

Llanberis (2004), **Ogwen and Carneddau** (1993), **Lliwedd** (1998), **Cwm Silyn** (2003), **Clogwyn Du'r Arddu** (2004) and **Tremadog** (2000). **North Wales Rock** (2009) published by Ground Up, offers a selected guide to the major crags.

Guidebook Footnote - The inclusion of a climbing area in this book does not mean that you have a right of access or the right to climb upon it. The descriptions within this guide are recorded for historical reasons only and no reliance should be placed on the accuracy of the description. The grades set in this guide are a fair assessment of the difficulty of the climbs. Climbers who attempt a route of a particular standard should use their own judgment as to whether they are proficient enough to tackle that route. This book is not a substitute for experience and proper judgment. The authors, publisher and distributors of this book do not recognise any liability for injury or damage caused to, or by, climbers, third parties, or property arising from such persons placing reliance on this guidebook as an assurance for their own safety.

High Mountain Guides

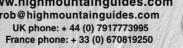

Tremadog | Cwm Silyn | Cloggy | Llanberis | Lliwedd | Ogwen | Carneddau | Betws y Coed | Welsh Winter

Route Symbols		**Crag Symbols**	
	1 star is good, 2 star is superb, 3 star is a classic.		Angle of the approach walk to the crag with approximate time.
	Technical climbing requiring good balance and technique, or complex and tricky moves.		Approximate time that the crag is in the sun (when it is shining!)
	Sustained climbing; either lots of hard moves or pumpy climbing.		A crag offering some shelter from bad weather.
	Fingery climbing with significant small holds on the hard sections.		**Deserted -** A quiet crag which may have a long walk-in and/or less good routes.
	Fluttery climbing with big fall potential and scary run-outs.		**Quiet -** Less popular sections on major crags, or good buttresses with long walk-ins.
	Graunchy climbing. Either wide cracks or thrutchy moves.		**Busy -** Places you will seldom be alone, especially at weekends. Good routes and easy access.
	Powerful climbing; roofs, steep rock or long moves off small holds.		**Crowded -** The most popular sections of the best crags. Classic routes and lots of people.

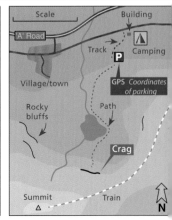

On the vast majority of routes in this guide there is no fixed gear, so everything you need to protect your ascent will have to be carried up the crag. This style of climbing is known as 'traditional' or 'trad' climbing.

Runners

A typical multi-pitch rack will be based around a double set of wires. These are your staple diet and should be supplemented with extras such as camming devices and hexes for wider cracks and micro-wires for some of the harder routes. It is also worth having a good selection of extenders or 'quickdraws' of varying lengths, and several 240cm slings. Many of the routes in this book weave around, and being able to extend your gear to avoid rope drag is essential. You'll also need a nut key to help remove stubborn pieces when your leader has put them in a little too well. Something you won't need is a guidebook pouch, as this book fits in your pocket!

Ropes

A pair of double ropes is needed for most of the routes in this book; 50m or 60m is the normal length. Some of the shorter single-pitch routes at areas such as the Upper Tier of Tremadog can be climbed on a single rope, but double ropes make multi-pitch climbing easier, reducing rope drag and giving you the option to abseil a full rope-length if needed.

Clothing

Any day out in the mountains of Wales can be a cold and unpleasant experience if you don't have the correct clothing. Waterproofs, warm mid-layers and hats and gloves are worthwhile additions to a pack and might make that 2 hour belay stint a little less painful. Having plenty of warm clothes to hand can be a lifesaver in the event of an accident too.

Further Reading

The Rockfax book *Trad*CLIMBING+ covers all aspects of traditional climbing including starting out, through gear, ropework and techniques, and on to more advanced skills like the mind and training. It is available from most outdoor retailers or direct from the online Rockfax shop - **www.rockfax.com**

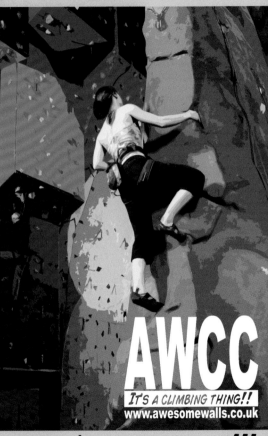

Tremadog · Cwm Silyn · Cloggy · Llanberis · Lliwedd · Ogwen · Carneddau · Betws y Coed · Welsh Winter

Classic Route	Page	British Trad Grade	Sport Grade	UIAA	USA
Little Tryfan Arete	120	Mod (Moderate)	1	I	5.1
Arete and Slab	111	Diff (Difficult)	2	II	5.2
Amphitheatre Buttress	160	VDiff (Very Difficult)	2+	III	5.3
Flying Buttress	91	HVD (Hard Very Difficult)	3-	III+	5.4
Crackstone Rib	87	S (Severe)	3	IV	5.5
Tennis Shoe	143	HS 4a (Hard Severe) BOLD / SAFE	3+	IV+	5.6
Grey Slab	141		4	V-	5.7
One Step in the Clouds	37	VS 4b 5a (Very Severe) SAFE	4+	V	5.8
Diagonal	97	HVS 4b 5c (Hard Very Severe) SAFE	5	V+	5.9
Fratricide Wall	174	E1 5b 5c BOLD / SAFE	5+	VI-	5.10a
Cemetry Gates	93		6a	VI	5.10b
Cenotaph Corner	93	E2 5a 6a BOLD / SAFE	6a+	VI+	5.10c
Vector	39	E3 6a BOLD / SAFE	6b	VII-	5.10d
Left Wall	93		6b+	VII	5.11a
West Buttress Eliminate	69	E4 5c 6b BOLD / SAFE	6c	VII+	5.11b
Great Wall	60		6c+	VIII-	5.11c
Right Wall	93	E5 6a 6c BOLD / SAFE	7a	VIII	5.11d
Cock Block	83		7a+	VIII+	5.12a
			7b	IX-	5.12b

British 'Trad' Grade

1) **Adjectival grade (Diff, VDiff, Sev, HS, VS, HVS, E1 and up).** How well-protected a route is, how sustained and a general indication of the level of difficulty of the whole route.

2) **Technical grade (4a, 4b, ... to 7b).** The difficulty of the hardest single move.

Colour Coding

The routes are all given a colour-code corresponding to a grade band.

Green Routes - Everything at grade Severe and under. Good routes to start on.

Orange Routes - Hard Severe to HVS inclusive. General ticking routes for those with more experience, a large range of excellent routes is available across this band.

Red Routes - E1 to E3 inclusive. Routes for the experienced and keen climber. A small selection of the best of these routes are included in this book for you to aspire to.

Black Routes - E4 and above. The hard stuff! There aren't many of these in this book.

BEACON
www.beaconclimbing.com

Climbing
Walls

Climbing courses for all ages, indoors and outdoors. Training courses for climbing supervisors.

Manufacturers of:
- Bouldering walls
- Roped climbing walls
- School traversing walls

Tel: 0845 450 8222
Email: info@beaconclimbing.com

Beacon Climbing Centre Ltd,
Ceunant, Caernarfon LL55 4SA

Tremadog

Cwm Silyn

Cloggy

Llanberis

Lliwedd

Ogwen

Carneddau

Betws y Coed

Welsh Winter

Shops

Joe Browns - Llanberis, Capel Curig. *See page 9.*
V12 - Llanberis.
Ultimate Outdoors - Betws y Coed.
Cotswolds - Betws y Coed.
The Great Arete - Bangor.

Walls

Beacon Climbing Centre - *See page 13.*
Plas y Brenin - *See opposite.*

Guides

ExpeditionGuide.com - *See inside front cover.*
Climb Mountains - *See inside back cover.*
High Mountain Guides - *See page 7.*
Plas y Brenin - *See opposite.*
Sea 2 Summit - *See page 17.*

Cafes

North Wales has a great number of climbers and a high annual rainfall, which means that there are a fair few cafes worth visiting.
Pete's Eats, Llanberis - Well known in this part of the world. A big menu of the old school. You most likely won't leave hungry. *Photo above.*
Canban, Brynrefail - A modern cafe/restaurant offering great food and coffees.
Pinnacle Cafe, Capel Curig - Found in the Pinnacle shop. All day breakfasts.
Eric's Cafe - Hard to miss if you're off to Tremadog.
The Big Rock Cafe, Porthmadog - On the main street of Porthmadog near to Tremadog. Home made cakes and good coffee.
Ogwen Cottage Snack Bar - Next to the pay and display car park at Ogwen Cottage, this snack bar gives hot and cold drinks and snacks.

Pubs

Good pubs are unfortunately quite hard to come by in North Wales, but here are a selection of the better offerings:
Vaynol Arms, Nant Peris - Opposite the campsite. Good beers and a pool table!
Plas y Brenin - The excellent bar in the centre is open in the evenings and has local ales, great food and a stunning lake view.
Glyntwrog, Llanrug - On the corner on the way to the Beacon Climbing Centre, this pub serves good food and good beer.
Pen y Gwryd Hotel, Llanberis Pass - On the far side of the pass from Llanberis, this old hotel has an excellent bar with log fires and a mountaineering history.
Bryn Tyrch, Capel Curig - On the main A5 road from Capel to Betws.
Does good beer and food and is popular with walkers.

Don't waste your time on home improvement.

If you want to improve your climbing rapidly, there's no better way than to get some professional coaching.

At Plas y Brenin our instructors are not only highly skilled, accomplished and experienced climbers, they're expert coaches too. They know exactly how to help you achieve your maximum potential as a climber.

Whether you're an absolute beginner, you've reached a plateau in your development, or you're simply ready to move up a grade and improve your technique, our coaches will help you improve - fast.

For a free 72-page colour brochure call us on 01690 720214, e-mail brochure@pyb.co.uk or take a look at our website at www.pyb.co.uk

Plas y Brenin, Capel Curig, Conwy LL24 0ET Tel: 01690 720214

www.pyb.co.uk

Tremadog · Cwm Silyn · Cloggy · Llanberis · Lliwedd · Ogwen · Carneddau · Betws y Coed · Welsh Winter

Writing this book has taken me to corners of North Wales that I may otherwise have missed and has allowed me to enjoy literally hundreds of routes (over a hundred in a fortnight during one summer!).

Countless people have helped me to write this book and listing them all would be impossible. I have no-doubt left out some people who really should be here, apologies for that!

Thanks firstly go to Alan James and Mick Ryan for all their help and support. Without both of them there would be no book. I'd also like to thank Ray Wood for his help with route info and also his superb photographs. Likewise a thank you to Mark Reeves. A big thank you to Sophie Evitt is in order for her invaluable help on the Carneddau and Tryfan sections, and also to James McHaffie for his attempts at helping with route info at Tremadog. I'd also like to thank Pete Robins for his last minute proofing and corrections.

Extra thanks go to the king of the Rockfax guidebooks; Chris Craggs, for his last minute additions and editing and the same also go to the new kid on the Rockfax block; Stephen Horne, for his work on the maps and text.

All the contributing photographers need to be thanked, especially Sean Kelly for his wonderful shot of the Trinity Face and Dave Dear for his shot of the Idwal Slabs.

Thanks to all the people who have let me photograph them over the last couple of years and thanks to everyone who belayed me or let me pass as I was soloing in my mission to document the route descriptions. A big thank you to Ian Wilson and Sarah Burmester for some great days out over the last winter and for agreeing to do one last route, just as the sun was setting.

Lastly, I'd like to thank John Yates for his help, advice and encouragement in all literary matters over the last few years. John, I owe you a lot.

Jack Geldard, March 2010

Tremadog

Tremadog

Cwm Silyn

Cloggy

Llanberis

Lliwedd

Ogwen

Carneddau

Betwys y Coed

Welsh Winter

Tremadog

Cwm Silyn

Cloggy

Llanberis

Lliwedd

Ogwen

Carneddau

Betws y Coed

Welsh Winter

Pete Robins places a cam on the tough E3 6a of *Neb Direct - page 34*. Photo: Jack Geldard

The fine dolerite cliffs of Tremadog flank the A498 Tremadog to Beddgelert road and are just a stone's throw from Eric's cafe and the parking. Facing south, at a low altitude and often spared the weather of the mountains, Tremadog gives year-round climbing on perfect rock with generally good gear and lots of three-star routes.

The high friction-dependence and extremely technical nature of some the moves mean that if you are not in-tune with your rock-ballet moves you might find some of the routes here quite tough. If you can revel in the hard grades, and enjoy being bamboozled, you'll have the time of your life!

Approach
From Tremadog, follow the A498 eastwards and the cliffs will be on your left as you drive past the large parking-area of Eric's Cafe on your right. You really can't miss them. The Upper Tier and Craig y Castell are both approached from the village of Tremadog itself, and the main venues of Pant Ifan and Craig Bwlch y Moch are approached from Eric's Cafe.

Conditions
The routes here dry quickly, get any sun going and are a good option when it is rainy in the mountains or you think you'll freeze on the high crags. In midsummer it can be too hot!

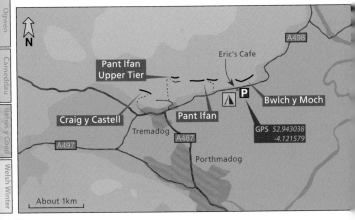

Craig y Castell

A fine crag, though the least popular of the Tremadog 'big three'. It faces south west and is a great afternoon venue. The tree cover and lichen ensure it doesn't dry too rapidly after rain.

Approach - From parking in Tremadog, follow the main road west to where a minor road branches right. Follow this past the school to its end then take the track on the right along the edge of the hospital. Cross the fence, head right a short distance then up the scree.

Descent - Scramble down a steep path to the right of the cliff.

CDW Direct (VS)
Lots of sun — 15 min

❶ One Step in the Crowds

. . . . 🎲①☐ E1 5b

A worthwhile trip up the left-hand side of the buttress. It gets a bit squeezed at the top, hence the name.

1) 5b, 28m. Start up the groove (as for *Creagh Dhu Wall*) but move left into the steep groove and up it to a roof. Move right then up to the big overhang then traverse out left, the diagonal crack in the roof helps. Pull left then back right to a small stance a little higher.

2) 5b, 28m. Cracks and groove lead to the roof. Pull over the right edge of this then move left round the arete for an independent finish.

FA. A.Evans, S.Beresford 1979

❷ Creagh Dhu Wall 🎲①☐ HS 4b

The route of the crag, great climbing up a big bulky buttress on lovely rock.

1) 4b, 28m. Climb the groove that leads to the overhangs and continue up a crack then make a delicate traverse right to a groove and soon, a large ledge and big fat tree belay.

2) 4b, 34m. Drop down and hand-traverse the huge flake out left then climb the face to a small ledge (possible stance). Step up and make hard moves into the polished slanting groove. Finish either side of the roof above this.

FA. J.Cunningham, W.Smith, P.Vaughan 1951

❸ The Wasp . . 🎲①✐☐ E2 5c

Quality and varied crack and groove work and maybe only E1 5b for grit aficionados. Start up the steep groove on the left side of the central bay of the cliff

1) 5c, 28m. Climb the groove then move left to a flake. The continuation crack is good value and needs a determined approach, as does the exit. Move left to a belay on *Creagh Dhu Wall's* beefy tree.

2) 5c, 24m. The long groove is technical, sustained and well protected to a leftwards exit - more full-on climbing.

FA. J.Brown, C.Davies 1960

21

① K.M.A. . . . . HS 4a
25m. Follow the wide crack on the left of
the crag to a grassy rest and a steep pull.
Step right on to the rounded arete to finish.
FA. C.Jones 1956

② Madog . . . . VS 4c
The twin cracks prove problematic.
25m. Follow the twin cracks to the steepening, pull through this using the wide crack
and romp up the crack to finish.

③ Myomancy . HVS 5b
A tricky start leads to easier ground.
28m. Follow the corner to the square-cut
roof. Turn the overhang on the right, then
trend back left and either finish direct or
join the previous route.

④ Falling Block Crack
. . . . S 4a
A pleasant and varied route.
25m. Totter up the rough arete to a ledge then
fight up the wide crack, with a hard move to
get established in the upper crack.
FA. C.Jones, S.Moore 1954

⑤ Mistook . . . . . . VS 4c
25m. Bubble your way up the strangely
pocketed rock to reach the previous route.

⑥ Gwynedd. . . VS 4b
25m. Technical moves lead up to and
through the sentry box. Follow the tricky
rightward slanting crack to finish.

⑦ Rammer's Route
. . . . VS 5a
25m. The thin technical wall just right of the
sentry box is climbed directly.
FA. G.Williams, A.Vereker 1955

8 **M.T.N . . . .** ☐ **S 4a**
25m. Climb the line of weakness on the right of the wall to gain the twin cracks.

Tremadog
Cwm Silyn
Cloggy
Llanberis
Lliwedd
Ogwen
Carneddau
Betws y Coed
Welsh Winter

Gwynedd

The Upper Tier of Tremadog is Wales' answer to a gritstone outcrop, but with better views! Mid-grade single pitch routes on perfect rock abound.
Descent - An easy walk off from the crag is possible at either end.

Lots of sun | 15 min | Sheltered

① **Bulging Wall** . . . ⬜ **HS 4a**

Good climbing up the step-like formations on the left edge of the tree shadowed buttress.
28m. Climb the steep rock steps and the wall above to reach an awkward groove. Pass this and follow the well positioned arete above on the left.
FA. T.Baugh, P.Baugh, D.Williams 1954

② **Quatre Fois Direct**

. . . . ⬜ **VS 4c**

The central slanting crack gives an interesting and gritstonesque outing.
28m. Climb the slanting crack behind the block in the middle of the wall to a ledge. Take the left-hand of the twin cracks above to finish or take a delicate line on the face just left of the crack at the same grade.
FA. P.Steele, T.Wright 1954

③ **Meirionydd**

. . . . ⬜ **E1 6a**

The fierce finger-crack sees more ascents at A1 than at E1!
28m. Torque your way up the lower crack on the right of the buttress. From the ledge take the right-hand crack in the upper wall to finish.

Meirionydd

The right side of the Upper Tier is home to an intensely technical E1 and a couple of other popular crack climbs on quality rock.

Tremadog

Cwm Silyn

Cloggy

Llanberis

Ll\iwedd

Ogwen

Carneddau

Betws y Coed

Welsh Winter

Stu McAleese cruising the top pitch of *Cream* (E4) - *page 39*. Photo: Jack Geldard

Tremadog

Tremadog
Cwm Silyn
Cloggy
Llanberis
Lliwedd
Ogwen
Carneddau
Betws y Coed
Welsh Winter

Abseil off

① Strapiombo . 🔆 👤 ☐ HVS 5b

A mighty chimney with moves to match.
1) 15m. Climb direct to a tree at the base of the chimney.
2) 5b, 18m. Get yourself into the chimney and use any means you can to get to the top. Breast stroke seems to work best.
FA. D.Whillans, G.Sutton 1955

② Poor Man's Peuterey

. . . . 🔆 ☐ S

A popular route in a good position. Start at the base of a groove with 'PMP' on it.

1) 20m. Climb the groove for 4m, move right and climb the arete to a tree (possible belay). Continue up the next groove above a ledge to another tree belay.
2) 10m. Traverse across the slab to belay in a corner.
3) 30m. Step right onto a nose of rock. Climb round the right-hand side of the nose which leads to the base of the upper slab (possible belay). Climb the slab then step right to a ledge. Scramble off above.
FA. G.Sutton, J.Gaukroger 1955

❸ Pincushion. . 🔲 E2 5c

A route of contrasts - it has roofs, slabs and cracks, wide bits, thin bits and blank bits.
1) 4a, 12m. Climb up grooves and easy rock to a tree at the base of a wide chimney.
2) 6a, 40m. Climb the chimney to the roof then make a testing move left across the slab. Pull up over the roof then climb a crack until a short distance below a roof. Move right to another crack and then right again at another roof to a final crack.
FA. P.Davies, M.Harris, R.Chorley (aid) 1956
FFA. H.Barber 1973

❹ Silly Arete 🔲 E3 5c

Probably the best line at Tremadog, and there are quite a lot of 'lines' on this crag. Immaculate climbing in a sensational position with more protection than you might think, but still very airy.
1) 4a, 12m. As for *Pincushion* to the tree.
2) 5c, 40m. Make a tricky step left onto the arete and climb this boldly to the overlap (long sling runner). Pull over the roof above the chimney on invisible holds, then move back onto the arete above and climb this to the top.
FA. J.Pasquill, J.Nutall. R.Evans 1971

❺ Fingerlicker . 🔲 E4 6a

Steep and fierce finger-jamming on pitch one, but perhaps not as hard as its reputation suggests. Start below the big corner of *Barbarian*.
1) 5c, 18m. Climb up left through a narrow chimney to gain the finger crack. Power impressively up this, not forgetting to place runners, to a small roof. Pull over, then climb up and traverse right to the belay on *Barbarian*.
2) 6a, 20m. Climb *Barbarian* through an overlap, then move left across the wall to gain *Silly Arete*. Finish up this.
FA. R.James, D.Jones (aid) 1964.
FFA. P.Livesey, J.Lawrence 1975

Scratch

A magnificent angular buttress with a set of classic corners and aretes.
Approach - Head up to the left-hand corner of the scree then through the trees to a clearing below the crag.
Descent - Abseil from trees at the top.

❻ Barbarian . . 🔲 E1 5b

The huge corner gives great climbing. Start by scrambling up to the base of the corner.
1) 4b, 15m. Climb the right wall then move left into the corner and climb it to a ledge belay.
2) 5b, 20m. Climb over the overhang then follow the corner until crack on the right lead to the next overlap. Pull through this with difficulty, then move up to a ledge (possibly belay if you are knackered). Step right and climb a groove to the top.
FA. C.Jones and party (aid) 1958. FFA. J.Brown 1960

❼ Scratch. . . . . . . 🔲 VS 4b

A delicate, easier route which is justifiably popular. Start below *Barbarian*.
1) 4b, 15m. Climb up and rightwards across the slab to a tree belay at the base of the upper corner.
2) 4b, 30m. Climb the corner then traverse right across the wall to a crack which leads to the top.
FA. A.Moulam, W.Craster 1953

❽ Scratch Arete 🔲 HVS 5a

The right-hand arete of the buttress gives a fine climb with a stopper crux. Start at a rib, where the approach path arrives at the crag.
1) 4c, 15m. Climb the rib and groove above to a crack. Climb this then move right to a tree belay.
2) 5a, 30m. Climb the slab on the left, then go back right to reach the arete just below the overlap. Step left and pull through with difficulty. Finish more easily above.
FA. B.Ingle, R.Jones 1962

Tremadog | Cwm Silyn | Cloggy | Llanberis | Llanwedd | Ogwen | Carneddau | Betws y Coed | Welsh Winter

Vulcan

The right-hand side of Pant y Fan is dominated by an immaculate wall and corner, in amongst some much poorer rock and above a bit of a jungle.

Approach - Head up to the right-hand corner of the scree then through the trees to a clearing below the corner of *Vulcan*. This can also be reached by a higher path.

Descent - Abseil from trees at the top.

Tremadog
Cwm Silyn
Clogwy
Llanberis
Lliwedd
Ogwen
Carneddau
Betws y Coed
Welsh Winter

Pete Robins on *Psych'n'Burn* (E6) - *opposite*. Photo: Jack Geldard

Scratch

Vulcan

❶ Psych'n'Burn E6 6c

Tackles the blank wall left of *Vulcan* by some extremely hard and harrowing climbing. High in the grade. *Photo opposite.*
1) 15m. As for *Vulcan*.
2) 6c, 35m. Climb the initial wall past loose fangs and bushes to gain a ledge. Micro wires and hard moves lead to crimpy holds and a peg. A very hard sequence leads past this to gain a good but hard-won wire. Continue straight up the slightly easier wall, trending right to finish.
FA. J.Moffatt 1981

❷ Vulcan E3 6a

This stupendous route is just plain hard. It tackles the slender groove running the full height of the crag via some intense and sustained moves and it regularly stops very competent climbers in their tracks.
1) 15m. Scramble up slabby rock below and right of the corner, then climb up, step right and then up to a ledge. Move up left to belay below the overhangs.
2) 6a, 35m. Climb up past the fangs then up the groove above. Step left into the main corner and make desperate layback moves up this to an overlap. Pull over this then continue up the still-difficult corner above to the top.
FA. B.Wright, C.Goodey (aid) 1962
FFA. R.Fawcett 1977

❸ Falcon E1 5b

A stunning route which follows the long, thin crackline right of the corner of *Vulcan*.
1) 15m. As for *Vulcan*.
2) 5b, 35m. Climb steeply past some fangs then up the groove above until it is possible to swing right around the corner to below the crack. Climb this all the way to an elephant's bottom finish.
FA. R.James, M.Petrovsky (aid) 1962
FFA. J.Clements 1964

Lots of sun | 10 min | Sheltered

A

③

①

Pippikin (E4)

②

Tremadog
Cwm Silyn
Cloggy
Llanberis
Lliwedd
Ogwen
Carneddau
Betws y Coed
Welsh Winter

29

Tremadog

Tremadog

Cwm Silyn

Clogwyn

Llanberis

Lliwedd

Ogwen

Carneddau

Betws-y-Coed

Welsh Winter

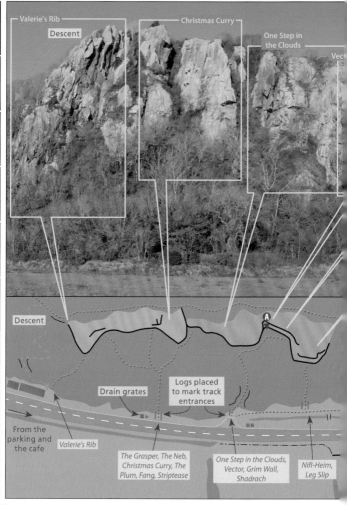

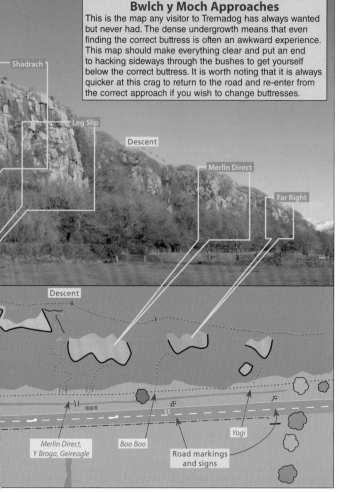

Bwlch y Moch Approaches

This is the map any visitor to Tremadog has always wanted but never had. The dense undergrowth means that even finding the correct buttress is often an awkward experience. This map should make everything clear and put an end to hacking sideways through the bushes to get yourself below the correct buttress. It is worth noting that it is always quicker at this crag to return to the road and re-enter from the correct approach if you wish to change buttresses.

Shadrach

Leg Slip

Descent

Merlin Direct

Far Right

Descent

*Merlin Direct,
Y Broga, Geireagle*

Boo Boo

Yogi

Road markings
and signs

Tremadog

Cwm Silyn

Clogwy

Llanberis

Lliwedd

Ogwen

Carneddau

Betws y Coed

Welsh Winter

31

Valerie's Rib . . . . ☼ ☐ **HS**

A popular route which makes the most of the broad rib on the left end of the crag.
Start at the toe of the buttress, below a large overhang.
1) 45m. Climb up left of the overhang then right to a tree (possible
belay). Move back left and up to a groove, climb the right side of
this and the crack above to a big ledge.
2) 30m. Scramble rightwards to a tree on a ledge. Climb
the crack above to another tree and then follow a
final crack and slabs to the top.
FA. P.Vaughan, W.Smith, J.Cunningham 1951

Descent

Valerie's Rib
A popular rib and the steep
face on its right-hand side
give two contrasting pitches.
Approach - See page 30.

Zukator (E4)

❷ The Grasper . ☼ ✐ ☐ **E2 5c**
The approach is a little awkward but the
final groove is well worth it. Scramble up
a steep vegetated path through the undergrowth to a sloping ledge below the steep
wall.
1) 5c, 25m. Climb up left, past a groove
to a niche. Pull out left again then climb a
groove to a small roof. Heave round this
then use a crack on the left to move up to a
well-positioned ledge-stance.
2) 5c, 20m. Move right and climb the brilliant groove with a hard pull to finish.
FA. J.Brown, D.Thomas (some aid) 1961

Lots of sun · 1 min · Sheltered

Tremadog · Cwm Silyn · Cloggy · Llanberis · Lliwedd · Ogwen · Carneddau · Betws y Coed · Welsh Winter

Bwlch y Moch

Trematog
Cwm Silyn
Cloggy
Llanberis
Lliwedd
Ogwen
Carneddau
Betws y Coed
Welsh Winter

Sally Ozanne stepping out on the exposed *Micah Finish* to *Christmas Curry* (HS) - *next page*. Photo: Jack Geldard

Christmas Curry

These two buttresses feature some great rock above some dense and sprawling vegetation. Great routes, including two of the most popular ticks in this book.

Approach - See page 30.

Tremadog
Cwm Silyn
Cloggy
Llanberis
Lliwedd
Ogwen
Carneddau
Betws y Coed
Welsh Winter

❶ The Neb Direct . . . . 🔲🔲🔲🔲 E3 6a

A great route with a fine open first pitch and a sensational and brutal final roof-crack. Start at the base of a gully, right of a corner. *Photo on page 18.*

1) 5b, 30m. Climb the steep, crozzly wall 4m right of the corner. Move right at 10m to gain the arete, climb it to a ledge and a short corner on the right. Climb this and step left to a tree belay.

2) 10m. Climb the short, easy nose of rock above to gain the large ledge. Walk rightwards along this and belay beneath the steep crack.

3) 5c, 6m. Climb the awkward and often-wet boulder problem crack to a ledge.

4) 6a, 14m. Climb the steep crack above the belay to below the roof. Jam easily through this and pull round the lip. Fight up the crack in the headwall to a tough top out and thank the Lord it was that short!

4a) The Neb - E2 5c, 18m. The original finish may provide a useful escape. Climb the steep crack above the belay to below the roof. Tiptoe rightwards under the roof until a smeary move gains the corner round to the right. Follow this to finish.

FA. (The Neb) J.Brown. D.Thomas 1961. FFA. (Direct) H.Barber, M.Lewis, H.Davies 1968

❷ Christmas Curry/Micah Finish. . . . . 🔲🔲 HS 4b

One of the most popular routes in North Wales with fine open climbing (and lots of people). Start below a short chimney. *Photo on previous page.*

1) 10m. Climb easily up the chimney to a tree belay.

2) 25m. Climb left to some sloping ledges, then climb up a wall. Holds on the right lead up before moving back left to a ledge.

3) 4b, 35m. Step right then climb a shallow groove to another groove. Climb this and a crack above to the arete. This leads to the top.

3a) Original Finish - Severe, 35m. Climb the slab behind the tree then step left above a small roof. Climb straight up to a good ledge (possible belay). Move across into a corner then pull out left to some spikes. Continue above up a groove to the top.

FA. A.Maulam, J.Barr 1953

❸ The Plum. . . . . 🔲🔲🔲 E1 5b

A brilliant route with a bit of everything. Start at the base of the gully, right of the arete.

45m. Climb a short corner (or come in higher from the right) and move left to a rib. Climb this and a short groove to a ledge (possible belay to reduce rope drag). Struggle up the wide crack above then move right and continue onto the arete. One tricky section up this leads to easier moves above.

FA. R.James, D.Yates 1961

Descent

The Neb Original

Christmas Curry Original (Sev)

1

2

3

Tremadog

Cwm Silyn

Cloggy

Llanberis

Lliwedd

Ogwen

Carneddau

Betws y Coed

Welsh Winter

One Step in the Clouds

Two distinct areas, each with a set of routes that feature enclosed starts in the undergrowth before reaching the open rock above.
Approach - See page 30.

Descent

Tremadog
Cwm Silyn
Cloggy
Llanberis
Lliwedd
Ogwen
Carneddau
Betws y Coed
Welsh Winter

Vector- page 39

Lots of sun
2 min
Sheltered

Pitch 1 shown on next page

36

Tremadog · Cwm Silyn · Cloggy · Llanberis · Llifwedd · Ogwen · Carneddau · Betws y Coed · Welsh Winter

❶ The Fang .. 🎖🗡☐ HVS 5a

Great climbing up and left of the huge fang.

1) 5a, 25m. Climb a crack to a pinnacle. Move left and climb a corner onto the arete. Move up and right to a ledge to belay.

2) 5a, 32m. Climb the wall on the left, then make hard moves round the arete onto the wall. Step left again then up and back right to reach the upper slab which leads to the top.

FA. J.Brown, C.Davies 1961

❷ Extraction 🎖🗡🗡☐ E2 5c

A fine counter line to *The Fang*.

1) 5c, 25m. Climb *The Fang* to the top of the pinnacle, then pull straight up the crack above and climb direct to the stance.

2) 5c, 30m. Move up right to a small ledge on the arete. Climb into a hanging groove above then make a hard pull out left onto the upper wall. Finish up the slab above.

FA. C.Phillips, M.Crook 1975

❸ Striptease . . . . . 🎖☐ VS 5a

The steep gully is better than you might expect and stays dry in light rain.

1) 5a, 40m. Climb the chimney and pull around the overhang on its right. Continue over more bulges to a tree belay on the right.

2) 4b, 12m. The short arete leads to the top.

FA. J.Brown, C.Davies 1961

❹ Hail Bebe . . . . . 🎖☐ VDiff

A fun way up the best cliff at Tremdog. Pitch two is a bit of a mud-fest but is more than compensated for by the upper pitches. The final teeter along the flake is a feast of exposure. Start below Vector buttress.

1) 10m. Climb directly up the steep blocky groove to gain the huge tree and a ledge.

2) 20m. Traverse left from the tree along the ledge, passing a single awkward step to gain a muddy, grassy ledge. Follow this for 10m to gain a good tree-belay.

3) 20m. Climb cracks directly above the belay to gain some good tree-root holds and a commodious tree (possible belay). Climb the crack straight above the tree with a tough move to gain the ledge at the top. Move right and teeter up the slab to another tree-belay.

5) 18m. Traverse right from the belay to gain slabby ground out on the nose. Move up to runners and foot-traverse the unlikely-looking large flake, fingers on slopy nothing, until it ends. Mantel on to the ledge, and either belay there and scramble the remaining 5m, or continue and belay on the top of the crag proper.

FA. A.Moulam, J.Barr 1954

❺ One Step in the Clouds

. . . . 🎖☐ VS 4c

A superb route with exposed climbing at a reasonable grade. Very popular and often busy. Start at the base of Vector Buttress (probably next to a pile of rucksacks). *Photo on cover.*

1) 4b, 25m. Climb blocks to a large tree (as for *Hail Bebe*). Move up and left to a short groove and climb this to a stance above.

2) 4c, 30m. Step left around the corner (possible belay here if crowded). Move right above the roof and then climb up the slab to a crack which leads to another stance.

3) 15m. Move right, then climb up to the flake. Either hand-traverse this to a final step to a ledge at the top, or do the easier *Hail Bebe* foot-traverse method to the same point.

FA. C.Jones, R.Moseley 1958

❻ Diadic . . . . . 🎖🗡☐ E1 5b

A pleasant, direct eliminate that includes the final groove of *Vector*.

1) 4b, 25m. As for *One Step...*

2) 5b, 30m. Make a hard move right, then pull over the bulge into a groove. Climb this to join *Vector* and finish up the crack above.

3) 15m. As for *One Step...*

FA E.Penman, A.Harris 1964

Tremadog

Cwm Silyn

Cloggy

Llanberis

Lliwedd

Ogwen

Carneddau

Betws y Coed

Welsh Winter

Descent

Strawberries (E7)

Atomic Finger
Flake (E4)

Hail Bebe and
One Step...

Vector

The most celebrated buttress at
Tremadog is home to many fine,
classic routes. They all follow
intricate and complex lines up
the buttress giving fine technical
climbing with big exposure.
Approach and Descent - See
page 30.

❶ Nimbus . . . . ** 🎩 🧗 ☐ **E2 5c

Relatively easy climbing with one hard move but in a great position. **The Snake** finish gives an even better combination at **E2 6a**.

1) 4b, 25m. As for *One Step...* (page 37).

2) 5c, 25m. Move up and right (as *Diadic*) but continue rightwards on the lip of a roof. Pull up with difficulty, as for *Weaver*, then break right up a steep groove which leads to the *Vector* cave stance.

3) 4b, 10m. Continue along the same diagonal line to the sloping ledge stance on *Void*. Either keep going to a tree in the gully and abseil off, or belay and continue up ...

4) The Snake, E2 6a, 20m. Struggle desperately into the niche and pull out. Swing left across the great headwall in a position of outstanding exposure - it was worth it!
FA. (Nimbus) J.Brown, C.Goodey 1961

❷ The Weaver . ** 🎩 🧗 ☐ **E2 5c

The most direct line on this complex buttress, despite its name!

1) 4b, 12m. Climb an awkward groove and short wall to the first *Vector* stance.

2) 5c, 35m. Traverse left, then pull up to join *Nimbus*. Climb through the bulge, then up left to a notch. Difficult moves lead up left, then climb fairly directly to the finishing flake of *Vector*.

3) 4b, 15m. As for *One Step...*
FA. C.Shorter, P.Williams 1980

❸ Cream . . ** 🎩 🪓 🧗 ☐ **E4 6a

A great finishing crack with good approach. Photo on page 25.

1) 4a, 10m. As for *Vector*.

2) 5c, 20m. Climb up, then pull left and tackle a short groove to join *Nimbus* pitch 2. Follow this to the cave stance.

3) 4b, 10m. As for *Nimbus*. The original line first traverses left then back right above the cave to the same stance below the crack - **6a**.

4) 6a, 15m. The crack is superb. Huge holds lead leftwards at the top.
FA. P.Livesey, R.Fawcett 1976

❹ Vector . . ** 🎩 🧗 🪓 ☐ **E2 5c

Possibly the most famous route at Tremadog. It is showing signs of over-climbing, and does get very chalky, but the positions and line are amazing. Start up and right of *One Step in the clouds*.

1) 5a, 15m. Climb a groove then step onto a slab on the right. Follow a corner up then move left again to the belay.

2) 5c, 25m. Polished and chalky. Climb up right to a difficult crack which leads to a spike. Make hard moves up to the base of the infamous Ochre Slab. Climb the slab then move left and up to an enclosed cave stance.

3) 5b, 20m. Traverse left then pull diagonally leftwards over a roof and onto another hanging slab. Continue left past more tricky moves to the final layback corner. Swarm up this to a comfy stance on *One Step*..

4) 4b, 15m. As for *One Step...*
FA. J.Brown, C.Davies 1960

❺ Void . . . . . . ** 🎩 🪓 🧗 ☐ **E3 6a

Another great route which is eliminate in its lower section but finishes in a superb position on the headwall. Start up and right of *Vector*, below a wide corner.

1) 5b, 12m. Climb the groove above to a spike belay (on *Vector*).

2) 5c, 20m. Join *Vector* and climb it through the Ochre Slab. At its top, pull right round a corner to a ledge. Move up right and climb a hidden crack to a sloping ledge belay.

2a) Atomic Finger Flake, E4 6b, 20m. The desperate steep-wall, which is the underside of the Ochre Slab.

3) 6a, 18m. Climb into the hanging pod with difficulty. Pull out left at the top then climb the crack with even more difficulty past a peg. Keep going up the crack and another crack on the right to the top.
FA. R.Edwards and party (aid point) 1975
FFA. R.Fawcett 1976

Tremadog
Cwm Silyn
Cloggy
Llanberis
Lliwedd
Ogwen
Carneddau
Betws y Coed
Welsh Winter

Lots of sun | 3 min | Sheltered

Descent or abseil

Void - previous page

A

A

1

2

3

4

5

Tremadog

Cwm Silyn

Cloggy

Llanberis

Lliwedd

Ogwen

Carneddau

Betws y Coed

Welsh Winter

1 Grim Wall Direct ☆☆ ☐ **E1 5b**

Direct but not very grim, unless someone abseils on your head, which does happen! Start right of the vegetated gully.

1) 5b, 30m. Climb a crack then a slab and then move left to a steepening. Pull over this then continue to a ledge and belay.

2) 5b, 25m. Climb straight to a small roof, then move right and finish up the wall.

2 Grim Wall . . . . . ☆☆ ☐ **VS 4b**

A good diagonal line leading to a fine finish. Start below the chimney of *Shadrach*.

1) 4b, 30m. Climb up left into a scoop. Move left again to a big flake and follow this to a small corner. Climb up then left to gain a small ledge.

2) 4b, 25m. Move up and right then pull back left through a small roof. Move left again to a rib then climb direct to the top.

FA. H.Smith, C.Jones, H.Fox 1957

3 Meshach. . . . . . ☆☆☆ ☐ **HVS 5a**

A popular climb with a great second pitch. Start below the chimney of *Shadrach*.

1) 4c, 32m. Climb up left to a small ledge. Go up a scoop and groove above and step right to another ledge. Move up again to a flake (on *Shadrach*) then step down left. Move up and then move left again to a corner and ledge just beyond on *Grim Wall*.

2) 5a, 25m. Follow *Grim Wall* over the small roof. Pull right onto another ledge and climb the wall above with difficulty (peg). Move left then back right to finish.

FA. R.James, A.Earnshaw, M.Petrousky 1962

Shadrach

A popular wall with some more amenably graded routes. The lines are intricate with good climbing especially in the upper sections. The view of people struggling on Vector Buttress routes is excellent from the top.

Approach - See page 30.

Descent - An abseil is possible from above *Grim Wall* or *Shadrach*. If people are climbing either route then the descent gully isn't far away.

4 Shadrach . . ☆☆ 🖐 ☐ **VS 4c**

A thrutchy chimney leading to more open climbing above. Another popular one. Start below the chimney. *Photo on page 3.*

1) 4c, 35m. The chimney is hard but safe, if you get in it, and easy but bold, if you climb the outside of it (possible belay). Step left and climb the flake and wall to a belay at the base of a big flake.

2) 4c, 18m. Climb the block then make hard moves to a shallow groove. Climb this then move right onto the final slab.

FA. A.Moulam, G.Piggott, D.Thomas 1951

5 The Brothers . . . ☆ ☐ **VS 4c**

A worthy alternative to *Meshach* and *Shadrach*. Start as for *Shadrach*.

1) 4b, 30m. Move right to a crack and climb this. At its top step down and then go up right to a ledge belay.

2) 4c, 28m. Move left past an overhang to eventually reach the *Shadrach* flake (possible belay - 4b). Finish up *Shadrach*.

2a) Direct Finish, HVS 5a, 25m. Climb direct from the flake past a small overlap to the top.

FA. C.Jones, T.Jones 1957

Leg Slip

One of the quieter buttresses at Bwlch y Moch with a set of technical groove climbs. The two *Slip* routes are especially worthwhile.

Approach - See page 30.

Descent - Walk right along the crag top to locate a steep descent gully.

1 Nifl-Heim . . 🔲 VS 5a

This makes the most of the left-hand side of the buttress. Start below a short chimney.

1) 4a, 12m. Climb the large chimney-groove past some alpine-esque blocks to gain a good ledge.

2) 4c, 15m. From the far left side of the ledge gain a right trending ramp-line (steep at first) and continue to a good tree-belay.

3) 5a, 12m. Pad up the slab on the right to gain a steep block-section and a junction with other routes. Climb up to an overlap and stride left, passing an old peg, to gain a breath-taking horizontal traverse on positive finger-slots. Follow these to a tree on the left.

4) 4a, 12m. Easy ground leads to a thin crack which is followed to a ledge and tree.

5) 4c, 12m. Climb the large off-width crack on the right. Luckily a parallel crack on the left takes normal sized nuts.

FA. H.Banner, E.Baldwin 1955

2 Pretzl Logic . . . . 🔲 E2 5c

A wandering route with a good finish. Start at a big tree just left of the pod of *Venom*.

1) 5b, 15m. Climb slabby rock to a small overlap. Make a baffling step left to bypass the roof and continue more easily up and left to a tree belay.

2) 5a, 30m. Move left from the stance and climb an inverted-V chimney to easy ground. Scramble up to join *Nifl-heim* and follow it to the stance below its top pitch.

2a) 5b, 30m. A good alternative. Climb up to join *Venom*. Follow its middle pitch.

3) 5c, 15m. Step left to a crack and climb this to a capping roof, pull over and finish up the short crack.

FA. A.Rouse, B.Hall 1974

3 Venom . 🔲 E3 6a

The smooth groove gives a superb, technical bridging problem.

1) 6a, 15m. Stem up the groove and exit left to the *Leg Slip* stance.

2) 5b, 25m. Climb up and pull-through onto the wall above. This leads past a small roof to a rightwards traverse and easier ground. Belay below the top chimney of *Nifl-Heim*.

3) 5c, 15m. As for *Pretzl Logic*.

FA. I.Edwards, W.Turner, P.Riley 1974

4 Leg Slip. . . . 🔲 E1 5b

Another fine groove climb with technical climbing and superb positions. Start below the prominent groove on the right of the buttress.

1) 5a, 15m. Climb the groove and escape left below the top roof onto the top of a sloping ramp.

2) 5b, 25m. Pull through the roof above into a fine groove. Bridge up this, moving right onto a rib then back left. Continue up the groove moving left around a roof onto easy ground. Tree belay above.

FA. J.Brown, C.Davies 1960

5 First Slip . . . 🔲 E1 5c

The right-hand *Slip* is even more technical.

1) 5c, 35m. As for *Leg Slip* but move right at the top of the groove to gain a ledge at the base of the beautiful upper groove. Climb this with sustained interest to good ledge.

2) 4b, 12m. Easy climbing leads up the arete and rough ground to a tree belay.

FA. J.Brown, C.Davies (1pt) 1960

Leg Slip **Bwlch y Moch**

Descent

Lots of sun | 3 min | Sheltered

Tremadog
Cwm Silyn
Clogwyn
Llanberis
Lliwedd
Ogwen
Carneddau
Betws y Coed
Welsh Winter

2

5

4

2

3

1

43

Descent - Head left over a stile then pick out a path leading to a steep gully. Follow it downwards steeply, passing some wooden steps.

Descent

Tremadog

Cwm Silyn

Clogwyn

Llanberis

Lliwedd

Ogwen

Carneddau

Betws-y-Coed

Welsh Winter

Lots of sun

3 min

Sheltered

Merlin Direct

An imposing buttress with a steep face and a polished slab. The easier routes see plenty of traffic.
Approach - See page 30

❶ Daddy Cool . 🎩 🧗 ☐ **E2 5c**

The vegetated bay has one decent route on its left-hand side. Start below the open groove in the centre of the bay.
1) 4c, 12m. Climb the left side of the groove to reach a ramp. Go up here to reach a tree belay in groove.
2) 5c, 15m. Move up the ramp onto a pedestal. Climb the crack above to an overlap, pull over into a diagonal groove and climb this to a ledge belay.
3) 5a, 12m. Move up and right, and then traverse across right into the corner.
4) 5c, 12m. Climb the corner with difficulty.
FA. D.Roberts, P.Williams, R.Edwards 1978

❷ Merlin Direct . . . 🎩 ☐ **HVS 5a**

Another popular route which sees plenty of traffic. Start below the big diamond-shaped wall, left of the slab.
1) 4c, 20m. Climb up left then make a hard move up and right up two cracks, into a groove. Climb this to a belay.
2) 5a, 25m. Climb the slab and crack to a ledge. Step left and gain a steep wall which leads to the top.
FA. A.Moulam, B.Gillott 1956

❸ Geireagle . . 🎩 🧗 ☐ **E3 5c**

Precarious balancy climbing up an over-hanging wall - how does it do that?
1) 5c, 38m. Follow *Merlin* to gain the ram-pline. Climb rightwards, then make some hard moves back left onto a ledge. Negotiate your way leftwards across this, then pull up and round onto the slab. Climb the slab to a belay.
2) 4a, 6m. Finish up the corner or abseil off.
FA. R.Edwards, J.Edwards 1966

❹ Vulture . 🎩 🖊 🧗 ☐ **E4 6a**

All the strenuous climbing that you would expect on *Geireagle* seems to have been transferred to this one. Very pumpy!
38m. Start as for *Geireagle*, but step up onto the rising line to gain the higher crack. Climb this, past the triangular niche, to join and finish up *Geireagle*.
FA. R.Edwards, J.Edwards (2pts) 1966

❺ Y Broga . . . . . . 🎩 ☐ **HVS 5a**

An extra-polished first pitch leads to more-open climbing above. Start by the slab below the big diamond-shaped wall.
1) 5a, 15m. The corner is slippery and awkward - big gear needed. Belay on a ledge.
2) 4b, 15m. Climb a crack to a ledge, then move up to another ledge. A short groove leads to a tree belay.
3) 4c, 15m. Climb the slab until tricky moves lead up left to gain the arete. This leads to the top.
FA. D.Jones, H.Morris, G.Williams 1962

❻ Oberon . . . . . . 🎩 ☐ **S 4b**

A varied route with commodious belay stances and a technical first pitch.
1) 4b, 15m. Climb the polished crack on the right of the slab, easing with height, to a step left which leads to the large ledge.
1a) 15m. The technical thin crack can be avoided by climbing the groove on the right - more in keeping with the rest of the route.
2) 15m. Climb the overhanging chimney above the stance to a steep squirmy move to gain a slab and a large ledge system.
3) 15m. Climb the slabby groove above to a slippery corner that leads to the top.
FA. A.Moulam, J.Neill, J.Glass, P.Chapman 1955

45

① Boo Boo Left-hand . . . . □ Diff

Delightful slab climbing on rough rock up a cleaned line. Scramble round to the left up a vague tree-covered path to gain a well-used starting ledge back right.

1) 25m. Climb up rough tree-root ground to gain the clean rock above. Climb the blunt arete on the right then the slab above to a reach good ledge.

2) 25m. Tackle the clean strip up the slab above to a ledge just below the top. Finish easily up the gully. Descend by walking left to the gully beyond Merlin Buttress.

FA. M.Edwards, N.Crofton 1961

Descent

Far Right

As the crag tapers off towards the ground there are a couple of decent buttresses sticking up out of the trees that give good, easier routes.

Approach - See page 30.

Descent - An abseil descent is possible from a fixed belay at the top of *Yogi*, with 50m ropes. Alternatively walk leftwards to the gully beyond *Merlin*.

② Yogi . . . . ☆① ☐ **VS 4b**

A technical first pitch gives access to the
well-positioned upper flake-crack.

1) 4b, 20m. Start at the foot of the arete.
Climb initially just on the right of the arete,
switching back left after a couple of metres.
Balance up the remaining arete to gain the
large ledge and good belays.

2) 4b, 25m. Climb the delightful slab above
the belay, heading to the rightward leaning
crack. Climb this and pad up the rounded
ball of rock to finish.

FA. G.Hodgkiss, M.Shannon 1961

Lots of sun   4 min   Sheltered

A

Easier start possible
on the left

2

Road sign is a good
location feature

Tremadog · Cwm Silyn · Cloggy · Llanberis · Lliwedd · Ogwen · Carneddau · Betws y Coed · Welsh Winter

47

Tremadog

Cwm Silyn

Cloggy

Llanberis

Llliwedd

Ogwen

Carneddau | Betws-y-Coed | Welsh Winter

Cwm Silyn

This fine mountain-crag features a wonderful slab of rock and offers a good set of routes across the grade range. The setting is magnificent above the twin tarns of Llynnau Cwm Silyn, and the delightful approach walk only adds to the day.

Approach
From Pen y Groes on the A487 follow signs to Llanllyfni, then towards Tan yr Allt. Ignore the first road on the right ('Tal Garnedd'), take the next right up an unmarked road parallel to a stream. Continue to the end of surfaced road and park through the gate in the field. Don't try and drive up the track towards the crag. From here a pleasant path leads gently up towards the two tarns. Skirt around these and tackle the scree up to the crag.

Conditions
The main slab faces south west but it is shaded from the sun early in the season. In the summer the crag makes a great afternoon venue when you may well appreciate why sunset ledge got its name. The main slab dries quickly after rain although there is some seepage towards its right-hand side. It is exposed to any wind.

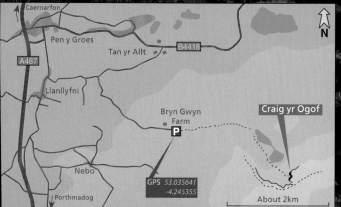

GPS 53.035641
-4.245355

About 2km

Afternoon

45 min

Descent

Tremadog

Cwm Silyn

Cloggy

Llanberis

Lliwedd

Ogwen

Carneddau

Betws y Coed

Welsh Winter

*Ordinary Route
and Kirkus Routes
- next page*

1

2

3

Approach

❶ Crucible. . . . 🔷🏃☐ E1 5b

A great route which takes an intricate line through the steeper lower walls of the buttress, culminating in some exposed moves around the big roof.

1) 4c, 30m. Climb the central of three grooves to a small overhang. Step right then climb up until you can move back left to a triangular overhang. Move left then climb up and back right above a roof. The stance is up and right.

2) 5b, 18m. Traverse leftwards to a block. Climb up the corner to a roof and pull over with difficulty to a ledge up and left. Traverse left to a corner and step down onto a ramp. Follow this across the steep wall to a belay above a groove.

3) 5a, 30m. Climb the groove to the top of a block. A rib on the left then leads up until you can move back into the main corner. Continue up this to a rest below the roof, then traverse right across the slab and up to the roof. Drop down right then reach up into a groove which leads to the Sunset Ledge.
FA. B.Ingle, R.Wilson 1963

❷ Jabberwocky 🔷🏃☐ E2 5c

This fine companion to *Crucible* has an excellent second pitch. Start below a short steep groove.

1) 5a, 30m. Climb the groove to a ledge then traverse up and left across the wall to an arete. Follow the arete to a ledge.

2) 5c, 30m. Step left onto the wall to a spike. Move back right to reach the main groove above. Tricky moves up this lead to a ramp on the left. Climb this to reach a small slab. Cross this to an arete, then move round into a corner which leads to Sunset Ledge.
FA. R.Evans, J.Yates, M.Yates 1970

Descent from Sunset Ledge - Either climb *Outside Edge Route* to the summit, or if you are confident, you could reverse solo down *Ordinary Route.*

Outside Edge Route

A superb wall with a steep lower section and slabbier rock above. The two routes on the left-hand side are both hard and strenuous, whilst the classic *Outside Edge Route* makes a great day out for those who like less taxing climbing.

Approach - See page 49.
Descent - From the top of the cliff walk rightwards. If you left gear at the base of the crag then you can drop down the steep gully right of the main cliff. If you didn't then you can enjoy a pleasant walk back home by continuing along the ridge path to join the main approach path.

❸ Outside Edge Route

. . . . 🔷☐ VDiff

One of the great Welsh mountain routes which takes a superb line across the buttress, finishing in a great position on the upper 'outside edge'. Start below a block roughly in the centre of the face.

1) 18m. Climb rightwards up a groove below the block. Move right around it and up to a stance

2) 25m. Climb up to a ledge then make a rising traverse up left to the arete. Climb this to a ledge and belays.

3) 18m. Move up onto Sunset Ledge then walk left for 6m and belay on the left side of the ledge.

4) 15m. Make as tricky traverse left around some ribs to gain a groove. Climb this to a ledge and belay.

5) 25m. Climb up and left to a corner-crack. Follow this (the crux, maybe a move of 4a) to the crest and a belay ledge.

6) 35m. Follow the ridge more easily from here to the top.
FA. J.M.Edwards, C.Palmer 1931

Tremadog
Cwm Silyn
Gloddfa
Llanberis
Lliwedd
Ogwen
Carneddau
Betws y Coed
Welsh Winter

Descent

Kirkus Route

The original route of the slab takes the easiest line up the middle, and further right are a fine pair of harder routes that make the most of the good rock.

Approach - See page 49.

Descent - From the top of the cliff walk rightwards. If you left gear at the base of the crag then you can drop down the steep gully right of the main cliff. If you didn't then you can enjoy a pleasant walk back home by continuing along the path to join your approach path.

5

6

4

Outside Edge on previous page

Approach

Tremadog

Cwm Silyn

Clogwyn

Llanberis

Lliwedd

Ogwen

Carnedd

Betws y Coed

Welsh Winter

Kirkus Route **Craig yr Ogof**

Tremadog

Cwm Silyn

Cloggy

Llanberis

Lliwedd

Ogwen

Carneddau

Betws y Coed

Welsh Winter

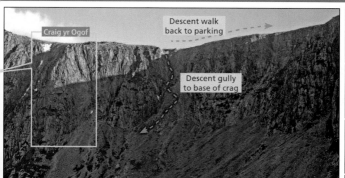

Craig yr Ogof

Descent walk
back to parking

Descent gully
to base of crag

❹ Ordinary Route . . 🔯 ☐ Diff
The original route of the slab is a fine route
which can be attempted in all weather by
the competent. There are plenty of ledges
for extra or different belays if desired. Start
towards the right-hand side of the face, by a
grassy pedestal.
1) 30m. Climb a wall then head left past several ledges to belay at the base of a groove.
2) 20m. Continue diagonally leftwards to
reach Sunset Ledge. Walk along this to belay
below a chimney/groove.
3) 25m. Climb the chimney/groove to a slab.
Continue up and belay where the angle eases.
4) 35m. Climb up leftwards to join *Outside
Edge Route*. Follow the crest to the top.
FA. D.Pye and party 1926

❺ Kirkus Route . . . 🔯 ☐ VS 4c
The original and easier of the pair gives good
sustained climbing that is never desperate.
Start as for *Ordinary Route*.
1) 4c, 30m. Climb the wall to ledges below a
forked diagonal crack. Climb the right-hand
branch of this into a niche. Continue to some
blocks above to belay.
2) 4b, 15m. Climb up a shallow scoop to a
groove which leads up and left to a belay on
a prominent break.

3) 4c, 15m. Climb direct past several overlaps to reach a good stance.
4) 4c, 20m. Climb up to a bulging section
pass this on the right and easier ground
leads to the top.
FA. C.Kirkus, G.Mcphee 1931

❻ Kirkus Direct 🔯 🧗 ☐ HVS 5b
A good companion which is probably less
direct than the original route. Start below the
right-hand side of the slab.
1) 5a, 25m. Climb a short slab (often wet)
then a steep section above. Gain and follow
a groove which leads up right until you can
swing left past flakes and drop down to gain
the stance of *Kirkus Route*.
2) 4c, 18m. Traverse left to reach a small
corner. Climb this then step right onto a rib.
Follow a crack and move left into another
groove which leads to the mid-height break.
3) 5b, 40m. A long pitch. Climb into the corner on the right and follow it to an overhang.
Move left to a crack and climb this then step
left at a mossy section. Climb the slab left of
the corner to the upper break. Move right into
a slim groove and climb this to the top.
FA. V.Ridgeway and party 1951

Tremadog

Cwm Silyn

Cloggy

Llanberis

Ll\iwedd

Ogwen

Carneddau

Betws y Coed

Welsh Winter

The Pinnacle

The Boulder

East Buttress

Clogwyn Du'r Arddu

Tremadog

Cwm Silyn

Cloggy

Llanberis

Lliwedd

Ogwen

Carneddau

Beaws y Coed

Welsh Winter

West Buttress

Far West Buttress

Cloggy bathed in summer evening sunlight. Photo: Jack Geldard

Tremadog

Cwm Silyn

Cloggy

Llanberis

Lliwedd

Ogwen

Carneddau

Betws y Coed

Welsh Winter

The big one. The most historically significant crag in Wales and perhaps one of the best climbing experiences in the UK. The rock is never quite dry enough, and never quite clean enough to make the routes feel easy. But on a day when the weather is just good enough to allow ascents to be made, it feels like you have taken a gamble and won. Cloggy is an amazing place.

Approach

Park in Llanberis and continue up the steep lane from the end of Victoria Terrace. Follow the road to reach the Snowdon summit path on the left. Follow this path for 3.5km passing the Halfway House Cafe. Where the main path continues up toward the summit, a subsidiary path contours rightwards to beneath the cliff. Follow this path to reach the desired buttress.

Conditions

The main crag faces north and only gets evening sun in summer time. Routes up on The Pinnacle get very early-morning sun too, but you'll still be in Pete's Eats at that time, surely? Cloggy is slow to dry, catches any wind going, and has a dusting of lichen that refuses to loose its grip even in midsummer. Don't let this put you off though; it's all part of the charm. Climb here on the warmest and driest days of the year, bring plenty of clothes and you'll have a fantastic mountain experience.

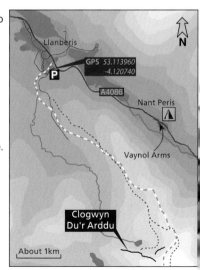

Llanberis

GPS 53.113960 -4.120740

A4086

Nant Peris

Vaynol Arms

Clogwyn Du'r Arddu

About 1km

Tremadog

Cwm Silyn

Cloggy

Llanberis

Lliwedd

Ogwen

Carneddau

Betws y Coed

Welsh Winter

Sean Villanueva O'Driscoll on *The Axe* (E4) -
page 64 - on the Pinnacle. Photo: Ray Wood

The Pinnacle

Pinnacle Arete - page 65

Pinnacle Arete - page 65

Chimney Route (VS)

1

2

3

4

5

Tremadog

Cwm Silyn

Cloggy

Llanberis

Lliwedd

Ogwen

Carneddau

Bethesda Coed

Welsh Winter

① Sunset Crack ... VS 5a
Good climbing up the prominent crack in a corner on the left-hand side of the wall.
1) 4a, 32m. Climb up to a grassy ledge below the crack (possible belay). Swarm up the crack to a belay below a steep section.
2) 5a, 20m. Make a hard move to gain the chimney on the lip of the overhang. Above, the pitch relents. Belay on the terrace and escape right.
FA. A.Cox 1937

② Llithrig E1 5c
A great, historical classic which traditionally involves a tension traverse on pitch 2.
1) 4a, 15m. Follow *Sunset Crack* to a stance below the corner.
2) 5c (5a), 18m. Move up and right to a groove which leads up to a ledge. Traverse right into a corner then pull up and right, following good holds to a spike. Make a very technical traverse across right (or tension off the spike at **HVS 5a**) to a belay ledge.
3) 4c, 15m. Move up and right to gain and follow a crack and corner to a belay.
4) 4c, 18m. Climb the corner then move left into a crack. This leads to ledges and the terrace. Escape off rightwards.
FA. J.Brown, J.Allen 1952. FFA. C.Phillips 1967

③ Pigott's Climb VS 5a
The original route of the East Buttress follows a series of huge stepped-corners.
1) 4a, 18m. Climb leftwards over ledges to follow a corner to a grassy ledge.
2) 4b, 15m. Head rightwards towards a corner which leads to another grass ledge.
3) 25m. Climb the corner and chimney above easily to belay on the large pillar.
4) 5a, 25m. The corner leads with difficulty to the top. An impressive pitch for the time.
FA. A.Pigott and party 1927

Pigott's Climb
It may be upstaged by its near-neighbour, but the area left of Great Wall has a series of worthy routes taking strong lines up corners, cracks and grooves at reasonable grades.
Descent - From the grass-terrace above the walls, scramble up and right to reach the Eastern Terrace, or move left with care and finish up one of the routes on the Pinnacle.

④ Diglyph...... HVS 5b
A good route that allows some of the aura of the Great Wall to be experienced at an amenable grade.
1) 18m. Climb the chimney, or the right wall, to a good stance.
2) 5b, 25m. Move right to a crack and climb this past a steep section (peg) and continue to a ledge. Belay on the right.
3) 4c, 30m. Climb up the wide groove above which leads to a large flake. Escape out right onto a steep wall to gain the terrace.
FA. J.Brown, M.Sorrell 1951

⑤ Daurigol ... E3 5c
A superb test-piece up the grooves on the left of the Great Wall.
1) 5b, 25m. Climb a groove left of a pinnacle then step back right and climb up to some breaks. Move right then up to a stance.
2) 5c, 20m. Climb up to the lower groove. Follow this until hard moves lead left to the upper groove. Continue to join *Diglyph*.
3) 4c, 30m. As for *Diglyph*.
FA. B.Ingle, M.Boysen (3 pts) 1962

Tremadog · Cwm Silyn · Cloggy · Llanberis · Lliwedd · Ogwen · Carneddau · Betws y Coed · Welsh Winter

❶ Great Wall

. . . . 〔3〕🔲🔲🔲 E4 6a

One of the UK's milestone routes for any aspiring hard climber. It takes a majestic line up this stunning wall with initially technical climbing giving way to easier, but bolder moves higher up.

1) 6a, 25m. Climb up to a small overlap below a line of cracks. Climb these with difficulty until a reach gains a crack. Pull up into to a depression to belay.

2) 5c, 38m. Climb the crack and then a corner above (becoming thin on gear). Make a long move to a good hold then traverse right and back left to easier ground.
FA. P.Crew 1962. FFA. J.Allen, C.Addy 1975

❷ The Indian Face

. . . . . . 〔3〕🔲🔲🔲🔲 E9 6c

50m. The Indian Face has established itself as *the* route of the 1980s. Two repeats in the quarter of a century since it was first climbed and no onsight ascents, despite routes with bigger E-grades receiving more ascents.
We haven't really included this route so that you should actually go and climb it, more to show you where it goes. If you are keen to make an ascent then we suggest you track down one of the previous ascensionists to get their beta.
FA. J.Dawes 1986

❸ November

. . 〔3〕🔲🔲 E3 5c

A magnificent, long crackline that defines the right-hand edge of Great Wall. It is good as described here but the *Jelly Roll* variation is probably the best, and it is a bit easier!

1) 5a, 25m. The drainpipe crack is often wet. This leads to a stance on the ramp on the right.

2) 5c, 38m. Continue up the increasingly-steep crack to a grassy ledge.

3) 5a, 20m. Climb the corner (tricky) then easier cracks to the Eastern Terrace.
FA. J.Brown, J.Smith 1957. FFA. A.McHardy 1970

Great Wall

One of the finest walls in the Country - this is the showpiece of the crag, a place of legends and myths, controversy and epics, triumph and failures. The routes are all magnificent challenges. A visit is a must for every climber.
Descent - Down the Eastern Terrace.

❹ Jelly Roll

. . . 〔3〕🔲🔲 E2 5b

A sensational airy line up the grooves above the *Indian Face*. Brilliant climbing at an unlikely grade for the situation.

1) 5a, 25m. As for *November*.

2) 5b, 18m. Continue up *November* until the crack closes up, then swing left and up to a ledge below a groove.

3) 5b, 35m. Climb the amazing groove above on big holds and oodles of exposure. At the top overhang, move left. Belay or continue up easy ground to the Eastern Terrace.
FA. R.Evans, C.Rogers 1971

❺ Vember

. . . . 〔3〕🔲 E1 5b

The original line using the *November* crack to start and one of the landmark routes of the Brown-Whillans era on Cloggy.

1) 5a, 25m. As for November.

2) 5b, 30m. Go right up the ramp to gain the chimney crack. This leads to a grassy ledge.

3) 4b, 12m. Climb the wall then easier ground to the Eastern Terrace.
FA. J.Brown, D.Whillans 1951

❻ Curving Crack

. . 〔3〕🔲 VS 4c

One of the older climbs up the huge curving groove on the right side of the buttress.

1) 4c, 10m. Climb to the top of the pedestal.

2) 5b, 18m. Traverse left into the corner-chimney. Climb this to a belay on the left.

3) 4c, 35m. Move back into the corner and follow it to the top.
FA. C.Kirkus and party 1932

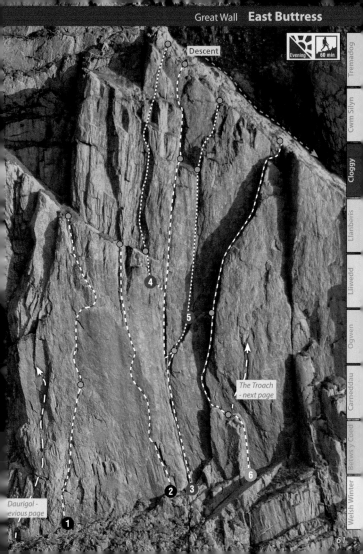

Evening | 60 min

Tremadog

Cwm Silyn

Cloggy

Llanberis

Lliwedd

Ogwen

Carneddau

Betws y Coed

Welsh Winter

Descent

④

⑤

The Troach
- next page

Daurigol -
evious page

①

② **③**

⑥

61

Descent

Curving Corner -
previous page

Tremadog

Cwm Silyn

Cloggy

Llanberis

Lliwedd

Ogwen

Carneddau

Betws-y-Coed

Welsh Winter

1

2

3

4

5

❶ The Troach.. E2 5b

A magnificent wall-route giving open and exposed climbing with adequate protection.
1) 4c, 10m. Climb onto the pedestal and belay, as for *Curving Crack*.
2) 5b, 40m. Move out right, then up via a hard move to a small ledge. Continue upwards past a couple of old pegs, eventually trending right to the large flake. Traditionally the belay is here, but continuing up left onto the arete makes for a better pitch and a more comfortable belay.
3) 5a, 15m. Finish easily up the arete.
FA. H.Banner, R.Wilson 1959. FFA. R.Evans 1967

❷ Pedestal Crack . HVS 5a

The middle one of the three long corners on this side of the buttress. Good climbing, but often a bit wet. Starting up the first pitch of *Scorpio* makes the route a worthwhile VS.
1) 5a, 20m. Climb the crack and belay on the pedestal on the right.
2) 4c, 15m. Move back into the crack and climb it to a stance in the corner.
3) 4b, 25m. Continue more easily to the top and a belay on the Eastern Terrace.
FA. C.Kirkus, G.MacPhee 1931

❸ Scorpio . E2 5b

A long pitch which tackles the impressive wall between *Pedestal Crack* and *The Corner*. Great sustained climbing leading to a thrilling climax high on the wall.
1) 4b, 20m. Climb the rib to a stance on the top of the pedestal.
2) 5b, 40m. Move right to a groove then climb this to a hand traverse. Move right along this then up to a ledge. Climb upwards steadily until a move right gains a blind flake. Sprint up this to finish.
FA. N.Soper, P.Crew 1961. FFA. T.Herley 1968

The Corner

On any other cliff, the walls and corners on the right-hand side of East Buttress would probably be the main attraction. Here they play second fiddle to the Great Wall - but only just.
Descent - Down the Eastern Terrace.

❹ Silhoutte . . . E2 5c

A great counter-diagonal to *Scorpio* which shares its middle section. Pitch 2 is long, so take a large rack.
1) 4b, 20m. As for *Scorpio* but move right to a stance below the wall.
2) 5c, 40m. Climb a thin crack to reach the groove of *Scorpio* (possible belay). Follow *Scorpio* to a peg, then move left and climb the crack, past a steep section, to the top.
FA. R.Edwards, N.Metcalfe 1975

❺ The Corner . HVS 5a

'Cloggy Corner' is comparable to *Cenotaph Corner* in quality but slightly easier. It is often wet but can usually still be done since the jams are all sinkers!
1) 4a, 20m. Scramble up slightly awkward ground, past grassy ledges to a belay on sloping rock below the corner. This point can also be reached from *Scorpio* pitch 1.
2) 5a, 35m. Climb the corner, fairly directly, with one slight detour onto the left wall at around 6m.
FA. J.Brown, J.Allen, D.Belshaw 1952

Tremadog
Cwm Silyn
Cloggy
Llanberis
Lliwedd
Ogwen
Carneddau
Betws y Coed
Welsh Winter

① Shrike . . . . . 〔3〕 🖊️ ☐ **E2 5c**

A superbly positioned route with massive exposure from the first move.

1) 5c, 12m. Climb a crack, then traverse left before tricky moves past a peg lead to a stance on ledges above.

2) 5b, 25m. Pull up the groove and over the overhang above, then move left to the arete. Climb up, then back right to the crack. Big holds lead up the exposed wall, move left and finish up the arete and wall to the right.

FA. J.Brown, H.Smith, J.Smith 1958

② The Axe . . . . 〔3〕 🖊️ ☐ **E4 6a**

The amazing arete gives a magnificent long pitch for which the word 'exposed' is nowhere near descriptive enough.
Photo on page 57.

6a, 35m. Climb right of the corner and make a hard pull over a small roof. Swing leftwards to a flake, then climb up to the arete above. This leads fairly directly all the way top the top. Sensational!

FA. P.Littlejohn, C.King 1979

③ Octo . . . 〔2〕 🖐️ 🧗 ☐ **E1 5b**

A great corner-climb, and as well-positioned as you would expect for this wall. The approach scramble across steep grass needs some care.

1) 4a, 15m. Climb the right-hand crack to a stance in the chimney.

2) 5b, 20m. Move up to an overhang, heave around this with difficulty, then climb the corner above to a ledge. Scramble off easily right to escape.

FA. J.Brown, Slim Sorrell, D. Belshaw 1952

The Pinnacle

A magnificent chunk of rock with routes that give stunning exposure and are well worth the effort of the arduous approach.

Approach - Abseil from a block on the right (facing out) of the East Gully. The routes are also often used as continuations of pitches below on East Buttress.

Descent - Down the Eastern Terrace.

Sidebar tabs: Tremadog · Cwm Silyn · Cloggy · Llanberis · Llilwedd · Ogwen · Carneddau · Betws y Coed · Welsh Winter

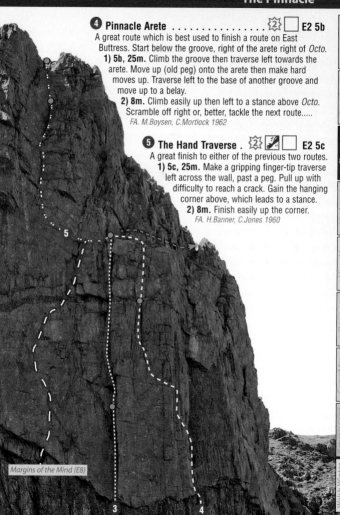

4 Pinnacle Arete .... ☆2 ▢ E2 5b

A great route which is best used to finish a route on East
Buttress. Start below the groove, right of the arete right of *Octo*.
1) 5b, 25m. Climb the groove then traverse left towards the
arete. Move up (old peg) onto the arete then make hard
moves up. Traverse left to the base of another groove and
move up to a belay.
　2) 8m. Climb easily up then left to a stance above *Octo*.
Scramble off right or, better, tackle the next route.....
FA. M.Boysen, C.Mortlock 1962

5 The Hand Traverse . ☆2 🪧 ▢ E2 5c

A great finish to either of the previous two routes.
1) 5c, 25m. Make a gripping finger-tip traverse
left across the wall, past a peg. Pull up with
difficulty to reach a crack. Gain the hanging
corner above, which leads to a stance.
　2) 8m. Finish easily up the corner.
FA. H.Banner, C.Jones 1960

Margins of the Mind (E8)

Tremadog

Cwm Silyn

Cloggy

Llanberis

Lliwedd

Ogwen

Carneddau

Betws y Coed

Welsh Winter

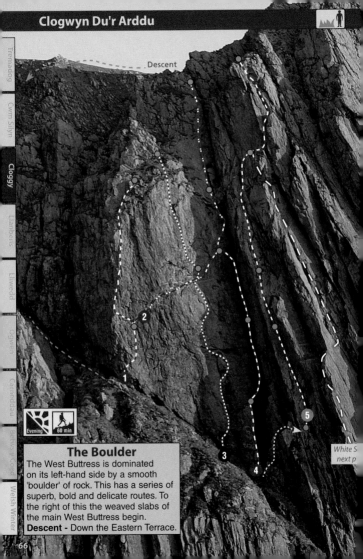

Descent

Tremadog

Cwm Silyn

Cloggy

Llanberis

Llïwedd

Ogwen

Carneddau

Holyhead / Gogarth

Welsh Winter

2

1

3

4

5

Evening   60 min

White S
next p

The Boulder

The West Buttress is dominated
on its left-hand side by a smooth
'boulder' of rock. This has a series of
superb, bold and delicate routes. To
the right of this the weaved slabs of
the main West Buttress begin.
Descent - Down the Eastern Terrace.

❶ Left Edge . . . 🏔️🗻☐ E1 5a

The 'easy' introduction to this slab follows the left edge as you would expect from the name. It gives amenable climbing with slightly spacey protection.

1) 4c, 15m. Step onto the slab and climb up to a small stance (peg).

2) 5a, 35m. Move up and left to a ledge and continue past a hard section to another ledge. Pull right then up to a short groove which leads to grassy ledges.
Scramble off above but take care when it is wet.
FA. R.Moseley 1954

❷ The Boulder . 🏔️🗻☐ E1 5a

A notch harder than its left-hand companion, it features a superb and exposed traverse across the face.

1) 4c, 15m. As for *Left Edge*.

2) 5a, 30m. Follow the gently-rising traverse line delicately rightwards. Move up to a stance just left of the corner.

3) 5a, 15m. Climb into the corner (*The Black Cleft*) then pull up and around the overhang above to a belay.

4) 25m. The slabby gully leads to the top.
FA. J.Brown 1951

❸ The Boldest . 🏔️🗻☐ E4 5c

The best of the bunch takes a direct line up the Boulder. With modern protection it is not as fierce as it was once thought and there is gear for the hardest moves.

1) 5c, 40m. Cross a grass ledge to a groove and climb this to a small overhang at its top. Traverse up and left to a small ledge then the wall above. Step right and go up to a flake. Put gear in this then head for the *Boulder* traverse. Belay a little higher.

2) 5c, 30m. Climb direct to a shallow groove. This gives some tricky moves before easier ground leads to the top. Belay well back with care.
FA. P.Crewe, B.Ingle 1963 (P2) C.Phillips, P.Minks 1969

The next two routes start at the base of the huge wet corner on the right of the Boulder.

❹ The Black Cleft
. . . . 🏔️🗻☐ E2 5c

Horrific and slippery climbing up the compellingly-obvious line - you have to *really* want to climb this one. The corner is usually wet in a summer drought, and really wet at other times so expect to get filthy. In winter it can offer a great ice route - **VII,7** mixed with thin ice on the first pitch.

1) 15m. Climb the right-hand edge of a pillar, left of the main corner and usually drier, and belay on the top.

2) 5c, 20m. Move into the corner and start swimming upwards to an optional stance.

3) 5c, 20m. Continue in the same damp line past some hanging gardens and a small overhang. Continue up then step left to a belay and junction with *The Boulder*.

4) 5a, 15m. Pitch 3 of *The Boulder*.

5) 25m. Pitch 4 of *The Boulder*.
FA. J.Brown, D.Whillans 1952

❺ Longland's Climb 🏔️☐ VS 4c

A fine old classic that takes an intricate line up the slender slab on this side of the West Buttress. The first route to breach the imposing West Buttress. Start at the foot of *The Black Cleft* and scramble across easy ground to a ledge below the corner proper.

1) 4a, 25m. Climb the corner to a chimney.

2) 4b, 12m. Climb up the chimney and slab above either on the left (easier) or by pulling out right and traversing back above (better).

3) 30m. Easy climbing leads up the slab to a ledge on the right.

4) 4c, 25m. From the right end of the ledge, pull up steeply then move right to a chimney. This leads to easier ground and the top.
FA. J.Longland and party 1928

Tremadog

Cwm Silyn

Cloggy

Llanberis

Lliwedd

Ogwen

Carneddau

Pass y Gwryd

Welsh Winter

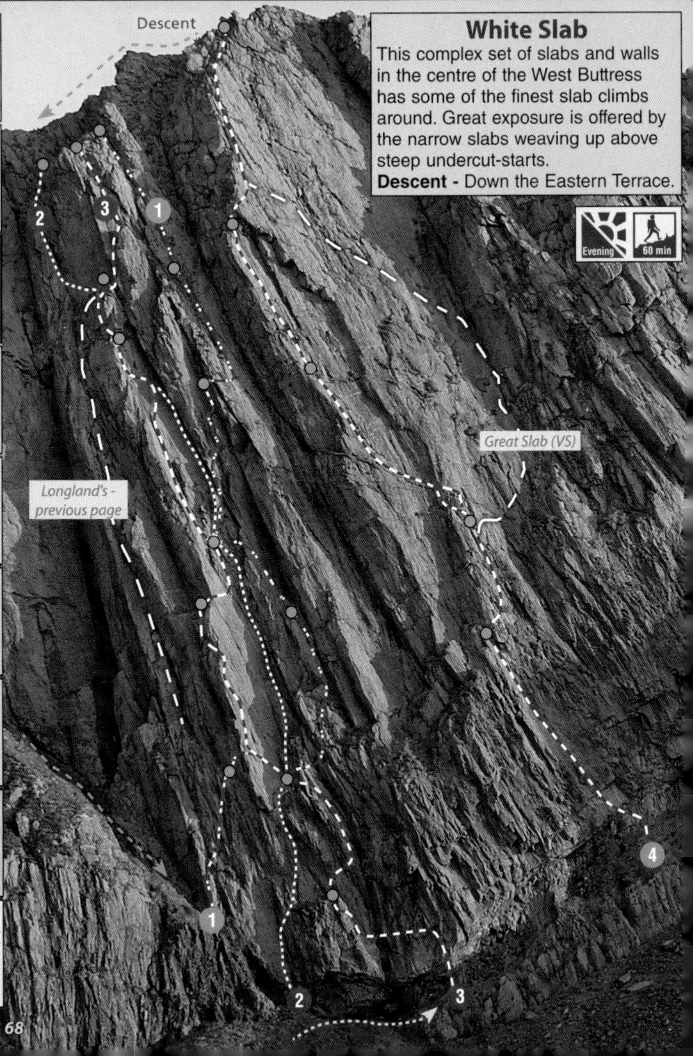

Descent

Tremadog

Cwm Silyn

Cloggy

Llanberis

Lliwedd

Ogwen

Carneddau

Betws y Coed

Welsh Winter

2

3

1

White Slab

This complex set of slabs and walls in the centre of the West Buttress has some of the finest slab climbs around. Great exposure is offered by the narrow slabs weaving up above steep undercut-starts.

Descent - Down the Eastern Terrace.

Evening | 60 min

Great Slab (VS)

Longland's - previous page

1

4

2

3

1 Sheaf .... ☑️ ⬜ VS 4c

A complex line that weaves up the West Buttress at a relatively friendly grade. Start at the base of the Eastern Terrace, just above a wet and grassy crack.

1) 4c, 20m. Climb a crack to a small stance under the rib of *White Slab*. This can also be reached from the base of *Longland's*.

2) 4c, 12m. Move right, then pull round onto the slab. Move right again, then descend with difficulty (Linnell's Leap).

3) 30m. Scramble rightwards then up grassy ledges to a belay in a corner.

4) 4b, 20m. Climb the slab to the arete and pull round to belay on *WBE*.

5) 4c, 20m. Move right then up the groove to an overhang. Swing round this to belay in the corner above.

6) 4c, 20m. Stride across the corner, then pull round onto a narrow slab. Climb this more easily...

7) 25m. ...past one stance to the top.
FA. J.Campell, A.Cox 1945

2 West Buttress Eliminate

.... ☑️ 🖊️ 🪝 ⬜ E3 5c

This superb climb takes the most direct line on this side of the West Buttress. Eliminate in name but certainly not eliminate in nature. Start below a red groove.

1) 5c, 35m. Climb the groove until you can move across the right wall and up to ledges. The groove above leads up with difficulty over a bulge to the base of the White Slab.

2) 5b, 40m. Climb the groove on the right-hand side of the slab. Belay on a flake.

3) 5b, 40m. *Walsh's Groove.* An amazing pitch requiring back-and-foot techniques. Very strenuous. Belay on *White Slab*.

4) 5a, 35m. Move left then up to a ledge (possible belay). Step left and climb the continuation of *Longland's* slab to the top.
FA. B.Ingle, P.Crewe 1962

3 White Slab.. ☑️ 🖊️ ⬜ E2 5c

One of the great Welsh Classics.

1) 5a, 35m. Make a delicate traverse across the lip over the overhangs to a groove.

2) 4b, 20m. Climb to the base of the slab.

3) 5a, 30m. Move up with difficulty to the arete (Linnell's Leap in reverse). Climb the arete to a spike, move right then back left into a groove. Move up to a belay.

4) 5c, 15m. Pull round the arete and make a thin traverse across the slab, then move up to a belay. Alternatively, lasso a small spike and tension across then up to the same belay (making the route a great **E1 5b**).

5) 5a, 35m. Climb the edge of the slab, detour right then back left and up to a ledge.

6) 4c, 35m. Move left then up to a ledge (possible belay). Pull up steeply then move right to a chimney. This leads to easier ground and the top - as for *Longland's*.
FA. R.Moseley, J.Smith 1956

4 Great Bow Combination

.... ☑️ ⬜ HVS 5a

A brilliant combination of pitches taking the best line up this side of the buttress. Start at a small pillar below a left-facing capped corner.

1) 4c, 45m. Climb onto the slab, step left to a groove which leads to a cave and ledge.

2) 4b, 12m. Pull around to the right then up to a stance.

3) 5a, 35m. Make a hard traverse leftwards along the break - low is harder, high is scarier. Continue to a crack which leads to a ledge on the left edge of the slab.

4) 4b, 25m. Steady climbing up the slab edge to another well-positioned stance.

5) 35m. Pull right back onto *Great Slab* and climb the rib to the top.

Great Slab - A great route on its own. Instead of belaying on pitch 2 above, break right across the slab to the far corner. This gives a few tricky moves before much easier climbing leads in three pitches to the top.
FA. C.Kirkus, G.Macphee 1930

Tremadog

Cwm Silyn

Cloggy

Llanberis

Lliwedd

Ogwen

Carneddau

Betws y Coed

Welsh Winter

Descent

Evening | 60 min | Windy

❶ Bloody Slab ☼ 📷 □ **E3 5b**
The finest route on the right-hand side of
the West Buttress tackles the clean red slab.
Approach - Start by scrambling high up the
Western Terrace to a point below the right
edge of the slab.
1) 5b, 30m. Pull up, then traverse up
leftwards to a flake. Move up over a bulge,
then continue up leftwards to a small overhang. Pull round this and belay in a shallow
corner (peg).
2) 5b, 25m. Traverse left and up to a rib,
then move left again to reach a grassy gully.
3) 35m. The rib above leads to easier
ground and the top.
Descent - Continue up the head right and
skirt around to the top of the Western
Terrace.
FA. J.Streetly 1952

Far West Buttress
Although not the same calibre
as routes on the rest of Cloggy,
the Far West Buttress has some
pleasant offerings at a friendly
grade. The slab can pretty much be
climbed anywhere at around S/HS.
Descent - Walk up right and skirt
down to the right of the buttress.

Approach
scramble

Tremadog | Cwm Silyn | Cloggy | Llanberis | Lliwedd | Ogwen | Carneddau | Betws y Coed | Welsh Winter

❷ Slanting Chimney ☆ ☐ S

The prominent chimney on the left side of the buttress gives a pleasant route when dry.
1) 10m. Start on the left and traverse in to a stance in the chimney proper.
2) 20m. Climb the chimney to a large ledge.
3) 20m. Continue finishing left of a large jammed block.
FA. H.Carr, G.Lister 1919

❸ Slab Climb Right-hand

. . . . ☆ ☐ HS 4a

The best line on the buttress, run-out in places.
1) 4a, 30m. Start at the toe of the buttress, climb up and right past a short corner, and onto slabs above. Continue to a grass ledge.
2) 20m. Move up and right to the main slab.
3) 35m - ish. Follow this past several ledges and belay where convenient.
4) 35m - ish. A similar pitch taking the line of best rock.
5) 15m. Continue to the top.
FA. G.Milburn, D.Gregory 1973

Descent

Tremadog
Cwm Silyn
Cloggy
Llanberis
Llïwedd
Ogwen
Carneddau
Y Coed
Helyg
Welsh Winter

Llanberis Pass

Tremadog

Cwm Silyn

Clogwy

Llanberis

Lliwedd

Ogwen

Carneddau

Betws y Coed

Welsh Winter

Kenji Iiyama on *Wind* (HVS) - *page 85* - Clogwyn y Grochan. Photo: Mark Reeves

Tremadog

Cwm Silyn

Cloggy

Llanberis

Lliwedd

Ogwen

Carneddau

Beddws y Coed

Welsh Winter

The Llanberis Pass is home to some of the finest and most famous routes in Britain. The accessible Clogwyn y Grochan and the essential Dinas Cromlech are amongst the most popular cliffs in Wales. The walk-ins are generally short, the routes are on good solid rock and are well travelled, and the ambience is that of good fun cragging. The south side of the valley (introduced on page 94) is home to a set of bigger, brooding cliffs with long routes and a mountaineering feel.

Approach

'The Pass' sits south east of the village of Llanberis, straddling the A4086. It is capped at its summit by Pen y Pass, the highest, and consequently very busy, parking for the summit of Snowdon. Parking is found for the crags in the many laybys up the valley. If these are full it is possible to park in Nant Peris and take the bus up the valley. The crags are usually approached directly from their closest layby via small paths.

Conditions

In the depths of winter the high crags of the Pass may have a coating of ice. In the warmer seasons most cliffs on the north side dry quickly (with the exception of Craig Ddu). The right wall of Dinas Cromlech often has a few wet streaks, getting in the way of many attempts at *Right Wall*, but the left wall of the crag, with *Resurrection* and *Left Wall* dries extremely quickly.

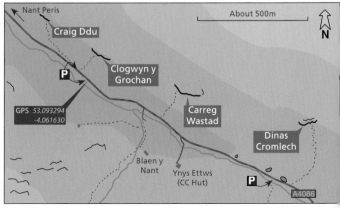

Side tabs: Tremadog | Cwm Silyn | Cloggy | **Llanberis** | Lliwedd | Ogwen | Carneddau | Betws y Coed | Welsh Winter

Tremadog

Cwm Silyn

Clogwyn

Llanberis

Lliwedd

Ogwen

Carneddau

Betws y Coed

Welsh Winter

David Ogden at the top of the majestic *Left Wall* (E2 5c)
- *page 93* - Dinas Cromlech. Photo: Mark Reeves

Black Wall

Yellow Groove

Lots of sun

10 min

4

5

Descent

1

2

3

Black Wall 20m

Black Wall
The left side of Craig Ddu is home to
several interesting routes. All are prone
to seepage and are in best condition
after a long dry period.

Tremadog
Cwm Silyn
Cloggy
Llanberis
Lliwedd
Ogwen
Carneddau
Betws y Coed
Welsh Winter

❶ Crown of Thorns

. . . . 🗒 🏞 🧗 ☐ **S 4a**

An interesting route tackling a great part of the left side of the cliff. Wait for a good dry-spell.

1) 30m. Start at a prominent boulder, 15m right of a chimney. Climb straight up to the ledge at 8m, then onto a rightward-leaning ramp. 7m above the ledge, at the top of the ramp, trend slightly leftwards and then continue straight up to another ledge. Follow the final rampline rightwards to a belay in the corner.

2) 4a, 25m. Skirt the steep wall above via a slab on the right. Pull back left and tackle the crux to reach easier ground.
FA. P.Harding, C.Noyce 1949

❷ Zig Zag . . . . 🗒 ☐ **VS 4b**

Another exciting classic taking an airy rising-traverse up the ramps and grooves.

1) 4b, 40m. Start below the square capping overhang at 6m. Zig up to a grassy ledge on the left at 6m, then zag back rightwards up the steep wall to another grassy ledge. Zig left into a short groove and keep heading left to the foot of a rightward-trending groove. Zag up this to a grassy belay.

2) 4b, 28m. Head up rightwards to the grassy ledge and aim for the black groove 5m right of the belay. Climb straight up to the top and belay well back.
FA. D.Belshaw, J.Brown 1952

❸ Canol . . 🗒 🍴 🧗 ☐ **E1 5b**

A fantastic excursion through the black walls of Craig Ddu, facing the challenge of the central and tallest section of wall.

1) 4c, 18m. Start just to the right of the overhang above the start of *Zig Zag*. Climb the black wall past small ledges for 9m. Step right and head up the wall to a block belay on the right.

2) 5b, 25m. Climb the steep wall on the left behind the belay and gain a rightward-trending rampline. Follow this until it butts up against a capping roof. Make an exciting pull through the left side of the roof and climb straight up to a ledge. Wander rightwards along the ledge to a block belay.

3) 4b, 20m. Step back left and climb the groove above the belay to the roof, which is taken via the large shattered weakness.
FA. J.Brown, D.Belshaw 1952

❹ Black Wall . . 🗒 🧗 ☐ **E2 5c**

A great route, best left for dry conditions.
1) 4c, 40m. Start at the base of the huge crack that makes the right-hand side of the enormous pinnacle. Traverse left to the arete as soon as possible, and climb it for 14m (possible belay). Climb the steep wall on the left to a scoop and head up and left to a small stance.

2) 5c, 35m. Climb the steep crack above until it reaches an overhang. Turn this with difficulty on the left side and continue straight up for 5m before a step right gains a thin crack. Strenuously climb this then follow a groove on the left to an overhang. Keep trending left across slabs (often wet) to a possible belay. Climb straight up from here for 10m to reach the top of the crag.
FA. D.Whillans, J.Brown 1954

❺ Rib and Slab . . . 🗒 ☐ **VDiff**

A fun route and a fine introduction to the crag.
1) 30m. Starting 20m right of the central pillar/crack and climb the large rib. Belay on an expansive ledge system.

2) 45m. Head rightwards onto the slab and follow it (keeping left of centre) to its top and a tricky belay. Close up photo of top section shown on following page.
FA. V.Wiggin, D.Meldrum 1948

Lots of sun | 10 min

Tremadog
Cwm Silyn
Cloggy
Llanberis
Lliwedd
Ogwen
Carneddau
Betws y Coed
Welsh Winter

*Rib and Slab
- previous page*

Descent

1
2
3
4

Yellow Groove

The right-hand side of the cliff is generally steeper and the rock can seem suspect in places. Don't let this put you off as the routes are quick-drying and offer fantastic climbing.

Descent - There is a gully 50m to the right of the crag that it is possible to descend. However, the easiest and safest option is to walk down the hillside on the left of the crag, past *Zig Zag* area.

Black Wall

Yellow Groove

① Rift Wall . . . 🏔️ 🧗 ☐ **VS 5a**

A brilliant route with a stiff crux.

1) 4b, 20m. Start in a bay, below the black grooves, 8m right of a fence post. Head easily up and left to a ledge, go straight up for 2m and then trend up and right to the base of the large slab. Follow the slab until a belay below the corner crack is reached.

2) 5a, 30m. Blast up the difficult corner-crack and follow the easier slab to a pedestal.

3) 4a, 12m. Head left to a steep corner. Make a flamboyant swing left on large flakes to gain the left arete. Finish easily.
FA. J.M.Edwards, K.Davies, F.Monkhouse 1949

② Orpheus. 🏔️ 🧗 🖼️ ☐ **E2 5b**

An exciting climb starting at 2 quartz bands.

1) 5b, 24m. Climb diagonally left to a shallow scoop (runner). Traverse right for 6m across the slab to a rest on the arete. Climb up on pockets to a step left into a niche. Step back right and pull through the overhang at the smallest point.

2) 4c, 15m. Climb rightwards up the short wall and climb easily to a small bay. From the right side of the bay move right and head straight up to the top of the pedestal.

3) 4c, 15m. Move right and climb the crack, passing an overhang. Follow the groove to the top.
FA. C.Phillips, R.Kirkwood, J.Arthy 1967

③ Yellow Groove

. . . . 🏔️ 🧗 🖼️ ☐ **VS 4b**

Superb and steep climbing through the imposing yellow wall.

1) 16m. Scramble up the right-hand side of the huge grassy rock-triangle to an ample block-belay.

2) 4b, 22m. Climb a groove to the large overhanging tooth. Step right and climb the continuation groove. A step left gains the straight-forward finish up the wall.
FA. J.Brown, D.Whillans 1955

④ Yellow Wall

. . . . 🏔️ 🧗 🖼️ ☐ **E2 5b**

A tough and sustained proposition with immaculate climbing and great moves.

1) 5b, 30m. Climb the wall just right of the large rock pyramid boldly for 6m to a rest and gear. Move up to a shallow groove on the on the left, which is followed to an overhang. Climb this (tricky) on the right and move up to a ledge.

1) 5b, 20m. Traverse left under an overhang to a sloping shelf. Pull rightwards through the roof above to gain a technical groove leading to the top.
FA. D.Yates, D.Potts 1962

Tremadog
Cwm Silyn
Glasgyn
Llanberis
Lliwedd
Ogwen
Carreddau
Betws y Coed
Welsh Winter

79

Tremadog

Cwm Silyn

Chegy

Llanberis

Llïwedd

Ogwen

Carnedau

Betws y Coed

Welsh Winter

Nea

The tall left-hand side of the crag has a long diagonal corner/groove running up it. This is the classic *Nea*. The other routes hereabouts give slightly steeper climbing.
Descent - It is common to abseil from the trees at the top of *Nea* - 50m to the ledge at the base of the climb. You can also walk down by climbing the wall behind the top stance for around 10m, then walk up and leftwards to gain the steep descent gully to the left of the buttress.

Lots of sun

5 min

① Phantom Rib . . . 🔲 VS 4c

A great and popular climb up a series of ribs on the left-hand side of the buttress.

1) 4b, 12m. On the wall are two parallel cracks. Climb them, then step slightly right, pass a tree and belay on the ledge.

2) 4c, 12m. Step up the groove and traverse right to the arete. Follow this (small holds and small wires) to a large ledge.

3) 4b, 18m. Follow the obvious corner until a step right brings you below 2 hanging grooves. Follow the groove in the arete, step right and climb to the large sloping ledge.

4) 4a, 14m. Climb the corner on the right, step back left then climb straight up to the large ledge (abseil).

FA. G.Pigott, M.Kennedy-Frazer, W.Stock 1949

② Nea . . . . . . 🔲 VS 4b

A classic outing, taking the central line of the buttress with some devious moves. Start on the large ledge gained by a scramble up the gully.

1) 4b, 20m. Climb the groove, taking the left branch until a precarious step back right gains a small belay.

2) 4a, 23m. Follow the obvious corner crack and chimney to a large ledge.

3) 4b, 20m. Pull left onto the steep wall and reach a small groove. Follow this to a ledge.

FA. N.Morin, J.M.Edwards 1941

③ Spectre . . . . 🔲 HVS 5a

The monstrous third pitch is good value HVS.

1) 4c, 12m. Climb the thin crack to a small ledge on the right, go straight up passing a large ledge to a tree belay.

2) 4a, 12m. Follow the groove above to the overhang which is passed most easily on the left. Head up and right to a belay ledge.

3) 5a, 18m. Climb the steep chimney crack! Finish as for *Nea*.

FA. P.Harding, E.Phillips 1947

④ Spectrum . . 🔲 E2 5c

A hard route with a steep start and a great second pitch.

1) 5b, 14m. Climb up to the shattered overhang and pull round this to a belay.

2) 5c, 30m. Move right and climb the superb technical wall to an overlap. Pull round this then head back up right and pull over a bulge. Continue more easily to the *Spectre* stance. Finish as for *Spectre*.

FFA. G.Regan 1978

Tremadog

Cwm Silyn

Clogwy

Llanberis

Lliwedd

Ogwen

Carneddau

Bry y G

Welsh Winter

82

Tremadog

Cwm Silyn

Clogsgy

Llanberis

Lliwedd

Ogwen

Carneddau

Betws y Coed

Welsh Winter

Brant Direct

The central section of the Grochan is fiercely steep. It has a few wandering mid-grade routes, but most of the routes are stiff challenges.

Descent - Most routes end at stances where an abseil is relatively simple to set up. For those who wish to top out, there is a walk-off descent to the left of Nea Buttress - see previous page.

❶ SS Special . ⚄ 🔨 ☐ E2 5b

Superb crack and face climbing followed by a stiff pull through the roof.

45m. Follow the right hand crack in the flat wall to a ledge. Take the thin crack above to a junction with *Sickle* at the roof. Pull through this to gain the right side of the undercut flake. Abseil descent, or continue up *Sickle*.
FA. D.Roberts, P.Williams, B.Dunne 1977

❷ Sickle . . . . ⚄ ☐ HVS 5b

A good route, but hard for the grade.

1) 5a, 20m. Start either side of the large flake. From the top of the flake climb the left wall via a thin crack, pass a ledge and head back right to a sloping stance.

2) 5b, 18m. Move left (tricky) to gain a groove. Climb this leftwards to the overhang which is passed on the left. Easier ground leads to a belay in the small square corner.

3) 4c, 18m. Trend leftwards across slabs crossing the gully and climbing a short steep crack to reach a stance on *Nea*.
FA. J.Brown, D.Cowan 1953

❸ Brant Direct
. . . . ⚄ 🪝 🔨 ☐ HVS 5a
26m. The central groove gives this classic bridging-route. Continue up *Brant* from the first belay.
FA. P.Harding, J.Disley, P.Hodgkinson, G.Dyke 1949

❹ Cockblock ⚄3 🪝 🔨 ☐ E5 6b
26m. A great introduction to the grade, with brutally hard climbing (RPs handy) to pass the obvious nut slot and a slightly run-out, but easier finish (small cam useful).
FA. J.Redhead, C.Shorter, K.Robertson 1980

❺ Slape Direct ⚄ 🔨 ☐ E2 5c
Short and fierce.
20m. Gain the leftward slanting crack from the right. Climb past a small quartz ledge and make hard moves through a bulge. Finish more easily.
FA. M.Harvey, D.Abbott (1pt) 1954

❻ First Amendment
. . . . ⚄ 🔨 ☐ E2 5c
The parallel line to *Slape Direct* gives a contrasting route.
1) 5c, 20m. The thin crack leads to a junction with *Brant*. Follow the groove above to a tree belay.
2) 5b, 25m. Follow the large flake behind the tree to a bold, smooth wall. Gain the groove and follow it to a ledge.
FA. D.Roberts, P.Williams 1978

❼ Brant . . . . ⚄ ☐ VS 4c
1) 4c, 20m. Climb into the sentry box and head left past a juggy spike. Move left along a ledge then go up a short groove and climb leftwards to belay at the top of *Brant Direct*.
2) 4c, 15m. Step down and left and enter the awkward v-groove. Climb this and head right along the ledge to belay in a corner.
3) 4a, 40m. Head leftwards up the slab, passing a corner and aiming for the large yew tree. A 60m abseil reaches the ground from here. A further 4a pitch up the front of the buttress above can be climbed to top out.
FA. J.Edwards, J.Barford 1940

Tremadog

Cwm Silyn

Cloggy

Llanberis

Lliwedd

Ogwen

Carneddau

Betws-y-Coed

Welsh Winter

Lots of sun

5 min

Wind

The ever-popular right-hand side of the Grochan sports several tough HVS's and a couple of belting E3 lines.

A

1

2

3

4

5

4

Descent - It is possible to abseil from the top of all routes described here. A VDiff ascent up and left can also be made from the large finishing ledge.

Brant - previous page

Tremadog
Cwm Silyn
Cloggy
Llanberis
Lliwedd
Ogwen
Carneddau
Betws y Coed
Welsh Winter

❶ Stroll On 🎯🗒📏☐ E3 6a
Pumpy climbing on good rock and gear.
40m. Follow the confusing lower wall to a
semi-rest under the small roof at 16m. Gird
your loins and tackle the roof (crux) and
steep crack above to reach easier ground
and a ledge.
FA. R.Fawcett, P.Livesey 1976

❷ Hangover 🎯🗒📏☐ E1 5b
A superb route with two contrasting pitches.
High in the grade.
1) 5a, 20m. Step right into the appealing
groove, and climb it boldly to a belay ledge.
2) 5b, 25m. Move rightwards round the arete
and climb the groove until it is possible to
move left into the final groove. Follow this
with difficulty to finish on a large ledge.
FA. J.Brown, R.Greenall, M.Sorrell, F.Ashton 1951

❸ Quasar . 🎯📏🗒☐ E3 6a
Short but steep, the crux holds on the
headwall sometimes seep.
40m. Climb the groove (surprisingly awkward)
to the overhang. Pass this on the right to
reach a good rest before the crux. Blast past
the crack above to reach *Kaiserbirge Wall*.
FA. J.Moran, A.Evans, E.Marshall 1977

❹ Karwendel Wall . 🎯☐ HVS 5b
A cruxy route with interesting moves on
good rock.
35m. Follow a shallow groove past a spike
to reach *Kaiserbirge Wall*. Follow this to a
sloping ledge from where a cruxy move gains
a hidden hold and a traverse-line leading
rightwards to a ledge and belay.
FA. H.Banner, J.O'Neill, R.Beesly 1958

❺ Kaisergebirge Wall
. . . . 🎯📏☐ HVS 5b
A great route that has the crux where it
should be... at the top!
35m. Follow the obvious traverse-line leftwards to a resting ledge. Attack the steep
groove on the left with gusto (crux) to gain
the ledge and belay.
FA. P.Harding, J.Disley, A.Moulam (aid) 1948

❻ Wind . . . . . 🎯🗒☐ HVS 5b
Another superb but tough Grochan HVS. High
in the grade. *Photo on page 72.*
27m. Follow the thin crack all the way to
belay on the ledge above.
FA. M.Crook, J.Moran 1977

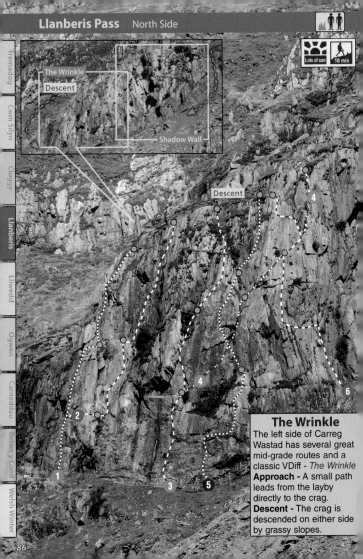

Tremadog

Cwm Silyn

Cloggy

Llanberis

Lliwedd

Ogwen

Carneddau

Betws y Coed

Welsh Winter

Lots of sun | 10 min

The Wrinkle

Descent

Shadow Wall

Descent

1 2 3 4 5 6

The Wrinkle
The left side of Carreg
Wastad has several great
mid-grade routes and a
classic VDiff - *The Wrinkle*
Approach - A small path
leads from the layby
directly to the crag.
Descent - The crag is
descended on either side
by grassy slopes.

❶ Skylon .... 🛡🧗⬜ HS 4b

A deservedly popular route following the left edge of the crag, with good gear and belays.
1) 4b, 37m. Climb to a ledge below a small overhang, move up right to a crack which is followed to another overhang and then a ledge. Head diagonally right to a terrace.
2) 24m. Climb the wall above the belay flake directly to a scramble finish.
FA. J.Handley, E.Phillips 1952

❷ The Wrinkle .... 🛡⬜ VDiff

A classic route on this great crag.
1) 24m. Start as for *Skylon*, but traverse right from below the first overhang to a ramp and then continue right to a good ledge.
2) 20m. Climb a crack at the right-hand end of the ledge. Move up rightwards then gain a groove leading back left to a slab. This leads to a good ledge with a big belay flake. The direct version of this pitch, up a steep groove, is also possible at about the same grade.
3) 30m. From the right-hand end of the ledge, climb up pinnacles. Then tackle the superb wobbly-jug-infested wall above to the square-cut top. Belay well back.
FA. M.Ward, J.Barford, B.Pierre 1947

❸ Unicorn ... 🛡🧗⬜ HVS 5b

A good, tough route with a tricky second pitch. Start below a groove, just right of the large overhang at 15m.
1) 4a, 15m. Weave up the lower wall to the large ledge.
2) 5b, 15m. Climb into the small groove above the ledge and make a hard move to gain the main groove on the left. Pass the trees to a good belay below an overhang.
3) 4b, 28m. Follow the groove on the right, then traverse right to a tiny ledge on the exposed rib. Follow the rib to the top.
FA. P.Harding, P.Hodgkinson, M.Hughes 1949

❹ Lion .... 🛡⬜ VS 4c

A classic Llanberis Pass VS and a good tick for any VS leader. Start as for *Unicorn*.
1) 4a, 15m. *Unicorn* Pitch 1.
2) 4c, 24m. Move right onto a black slab, continue diagonally right to an overlap. Keep going up and right to the large fissure of **Overhanging Chimney (VS)** and climb this past a chockstone until a swing right on the wall leads to a stance.
3) 26m. Climb the slab on the right, pass a short chimney, continue on to *Crackstone Rib*.
4) 4a, 18m. Step right from the stance and climb up to a tree, then follow a large flake.
FA. P.Harding, A.Moulam 1948

❺ Overlapping Wall 🛡⬜ E1 5b

An exciting route with memorable moments.
1) 4c, 27m. Tackle the wall left of the large overhang for 6m then traverse right to a ledge. Continue straight up to a stance below the chockstone of **Overhanging Chimney (VS)**.
2) 5b, 21m. Start up the groove, then gain the left arete. Head left, passing the overlap and continue left until a groove leads back right to a ledge, then a corner and a belay.
3) 4c, 27m. Traverse up and right across the wall to gain the final exposed rib.
FA. M.Hughes 1948

❻ Crackstone Rib .. 🛡⬜ S 4a

Fantastic rock and positions make this a must do route whatever grade you climb.
1) 35m. Climb the wide chimney to a ledge, then follow a well-trodden traverse-line left to the arete. Swing boldly onto the arete and follow it to a ledge. Take the short wall above to a sloping ledge to belay.
2) 4a, 20m. Climb up easily right to a corner, then climb up and make a tricky traverse left to finish up a short crack.
FA. J.M.Edwards, J.Joyce 1935

Tremadog

Cwm Silyn

Cloggy

Llanberis

Lliwedd

Ogwen

Carneddau

Betws y Coed

Welsh Winter

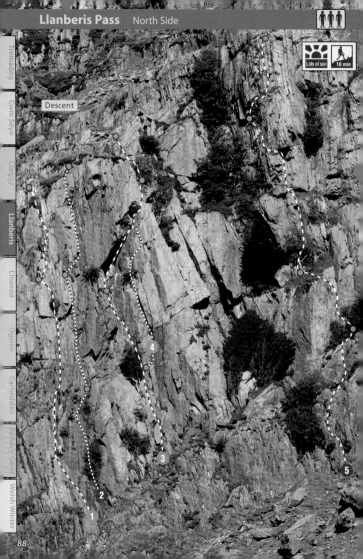

Llanberis Pass   North Side

Tremadog

Cwm Silyn

Cloggy

Llanberis

Lliwedd

Ogwen

Carneddau

BEWS y Coed

Welsh Winter

Lots of sun   10 min

Descent

4

3

2

1

5

❶ Ribstone Crack

. . . . 🏔2 🔦 ☐ **VS 4c**

A classic beefy pitch that requires a bit of grunt!

1) 4c, 34m. Start as for *Crackstone Rib*, up the crack to gain the ledge. Stride right and meet the impending crack head on. Jam, layback and improvise up this until a swing left gains a sloping belay ledge.

2) 4a, 18m. Swing back right and follow the large flake all the way to the top.
FA. J.Disley, A.Moulam 1951

❷ Erosion Groove Direct

. . . . 🏔 🪛 🖉 ☐ **E2 5c**

A direct and tricky pitch on which good technique and a bit of arm power are needed.

1) 15m. Scramble up past a holly tree, then continue on the wall on the left to gain a stance on a large flake.

2) 5a, 20m. Gain the corner via some tricky moves and follow it, passing right of an overlap at 15m, to a good stance.

3) 5c, 20m. The crux comes after a step right, gaining the groove is problematical, but a wide crack above relents slightly, and hopefully leads to the top.
FA. D.Whillans, J.Brown 1955

❸ Shadow Wall 🏔3 🪛 ☐ **VS 4c**

Don't be put off by the scrappy start, the traverse under the roof is not to be missed.

1) 4a, 27m. Scramble up the groove to the large tree (possible belay) and continue up the groove to belay under the roof.

2) 4c, 15m. Follow the line below the rightward slanting roof with difficulty to a small groove. Follow this to a stance at a tree.

3) 8m. Climb easily up to the ledge.
FA. J.M.Edwards, J.Boyce 1935

Shadow Wall

The right side of Carreg Wastad has some steep and burly routes that will test both bicep and brain. *Shadow Wall* and *Old Holborn* being two of the best.

Descent - The crag is descended on either side by grassy slopes.

---

❹ Yellow Crack 🏔 🔦 ☐ **HVS 5b**

A big tough crack for big tough climbers!

1) 12m. Climb the lower groove of *Shadow Wall* to the first large tree, belay.

2) 5b, 30m. Step right and launch up the steep corner-crack to a ledge. Step right into a groove then back left to join *Shadow Wall*.

3) 8m. As for the final pitch of *Shadow Wall*.
FA. H.Banner, C.Jones 1958

❺ Old Holborn 🏔 💬 ☐ **E1 5b**

A superbly exposed finale makes this a tremendous outing.

1) 4c, 27m. Start at a small rib flanked on both sides by grooves. Climb the groove on the right of the rib, then surmount the rib itself. From its top, move right onto a slanting rake. Follow this to belay in the holly trees.

2) 4a, 9m. Follow the short groove on the left side of the ledge, passing a detached flake to gain a large ledge and tree belay.

3) 5b, 27m. THE pitch! A superbly sustained groove above the belay leads to a step right. Pass a loose block with care to reach the large roof above. A wild monkey-swing through the roof gains a hidden ledge. Follow the steep arete above to small ledges and interesting belays.

4) 4c, 18m. Trend rightwards up the steep face with sparse protection.
FA. P.Crew, B.Ingle, D.Potts 1963

Tremadog

Cwm Silyn

Cloggy

Llanberis

Lliwedd

Ogwen

Carneddau

Betws y Coed

Welsh Winter

Lots of sun

20 min

Tremadog

Cwm Silyn

Clogwy

Llanberis

Lliwedd

Ogwen

Carneddau

Betws-y-Coed

Welsh Winter

Descent

Cenotaph Corner
- next page

Foil (E3)

Memory
Lane (E3)

2

The Forest

4

Approach scrambl

2   3

1   2   3

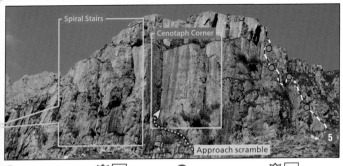

1 Noah's Warning . ⬡ ☐ VS 5a

A superb route that is high in the grade.
1) **4c, 40m.** Follow the striking crack, turning a tricky bulge on the left to reach a ledge.
2) **5a, 28m.** Follow the wide crack above to a steep flake. Move right into a faint scoop and head up to a thin crack. Scramble or climb off as for *Spiral Stairs*.
FA. J.Brown, M.Sorrell 1951

2 Dives/Better Things

. . . . ⬡ 🧗 ☐ HS 4b

A top class route with a thrilling finale.
1) **4a, 25m.** A steep crack gives access to a rightward traverse on pocketed rock beneath the large roof (often wet). Belay at *The Forest*.
2) **4b, 24m.** Traverse out leftwards to reach the superb corner crack and follow it throughout.
FA. (Dives) J.M.Edwards 1949
FA. (Better Things) T.Bourdillon, J.Tomlinson 1949

3 Sabre Cut . ⬡ 👊 ☐ VS 4c

Another Llanberis Pass classic.
1) **4c, 32m.** Climb the corner, then head right over vegetated ground to *The Forest*.
2) **4b, 25m.** Follow the easier but wide and sustained corner-crack to the top.
FA. E.Williams, R.Williams 1935

Foil (E3) *takes the thin crack on the right above the belay ledge of The Forest.*

4 Spiral Stairs. . . . ⬡ ☐ VDiff

A wonderful adventure spiralling across some impressive terrain.
1) **20m.** From the base of the sloping ledge under Cenotaph Corner, climb polished flakes up and then leftwards until an airy step down (tricky to protect the second) reaches the arete. Keep trending left, passing a huge flake, to reach the ledge known as *The Forest*.
2) **22m.** Climb up left to the steep crack. Pull up this to a ledge and climb the easier slab on the left to a sloping belay ledge.
3) **25m.** The wide chimney crack gives access to an easy slab. Walk along this and ascend a large groove on the right to finish.
FA. J.M.Edwards, S.Darbishire 1931

*The classic **Memory Lane (E3)** follows the airy arete above the first pitch of Spiral Stairs.*

5 Flying Buttress . . ⬡ ☐ VDiff

Start just right of the large white quartz slab.
1) **16m.** Head up the middle of the buttress.
2) **18m.** Continue up to the large pinnacles.
3) **20m.** Drop down in the gap and climb the steep wall on the left.
4) **15m.** Follow the slab rightwards to a ledge.
5) **15m.** The polished, awkward chimney on the right is thankfully short-lived!
FA. J.M.Edwards 1931

Cenotaph Corner

Approach - A short scramble leads to a ledge below the routes.
Descent - Fixed abseil stations are found on the top of most routes. Beware of climbers below when abseiling.

Lord of the Flies (E6)

Porthole

Tremadog

Cwm Silyn

Cloggy

Llanberis

Lilwedd

Ogwen

Carnedau

Betws y Coed

Welsh Winter

2

1   **3**   **4**   **5**   **6**

92

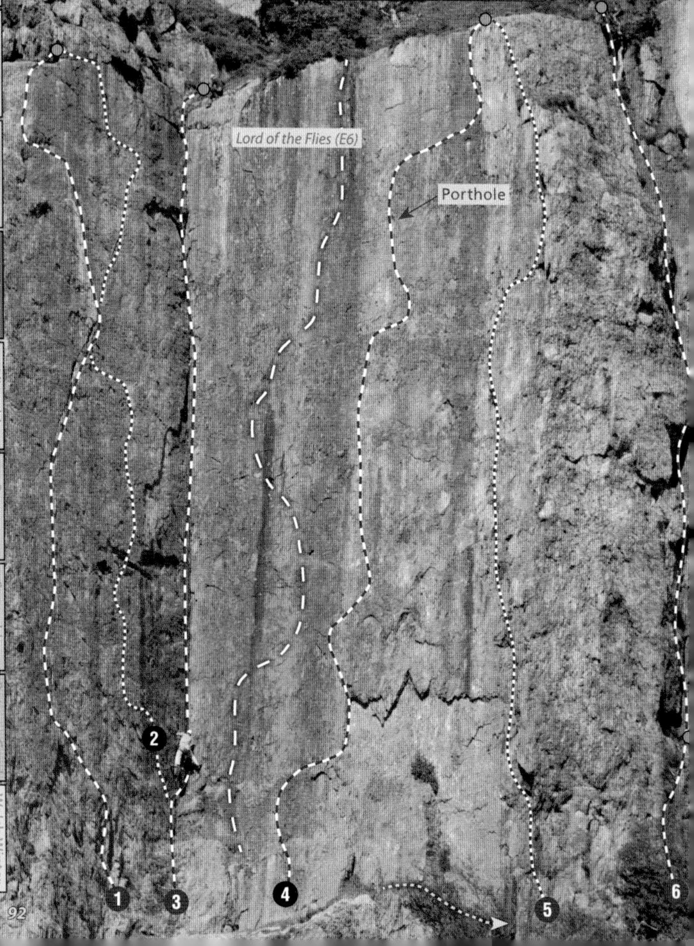

❶ Left Wall . . . 　 E2 5c

Quite simply one of the best pitches in Britain; good gear, great climbing and an amazing position. *Photo on page 75.*

40m. Fire up the initial steep crack, passing a surprisingly tricky move, to gain a semi-rest below the grand finale; the leftward-slanting thin crack. Follow this to a line of slightly crumbly juggy flakes leading horizontally left. Finish easily up the arete.

FA. R.Moseley, J.Smith, J.Sutherland (aid) 1956
FFA. A.Garlick 1970

❷ Resurrection

. . . . 　 E4 6a

They say it's harder than *Right Wall*, but at least it has gear! The final wall sees many wobbling leaders as arms start to fade fast.

40m. Start on large holds just left of *Cenotaph Corner*, passing a (sometimes) insitu thread. Long moves (peg) lead to an easier traverse left to join *Left Wall*. Sprint up the right-hand crackline and stuff it full of gear. Take a deep breath, step left and finish boldly up the wall. An alternative finish is to follow the crackline up rightwards, past a flat hold, to the top - about the same difficulty.

FA. R.Edwards, D.Belshaw (4pts) 1975
FFA. P.Livesey, J.Lawrence 1975

❸ Cenotaph Corner

. . . . 　 E1 5c

The line of the country, and a milestone in every British climber's career.

40m. Follow the striking open-book corner with increasing difficulty to a tough crux right at the top. An ancient peg sits below the final hard section - it is wise to back this up!

FA. J.Brown, D.Belshaw (2pts) 1952

*Just right of the corner is the line of **Lord of the Flies (E6 6a)**, made famous by Ron Fawcett on the TV series Rock Athlete. "Come on arms, do your stuff!"*

❹ Right Wall

. . . . . 　 E5 6a

A classic bold wall-climb, weaving its way up the stunning wall right of *Cenotaph Corner*.

40m. Climb up to the leftward-slanting crack by an undercut at 5m. Follow this crack for 2m, then head up and right to the first ledge. Follow a line of crozzly pockets up the wall above to reach the girdle ledge. Step slightly right, arrange crucial protection and climb the wall leftwards to the 'porthole'. Pass this, all guns blazing, and aim for the safety of the final ledge above. Walk rightwards and finish up the crack.

FA. P.Livesey 1974

Climb rightwards off the ledge, heading down behind the large flake to reach the next routes.

❺ Cemetery Gates

. . . . 　 E1 5b

The easiest of the three E1's, but no push-over. The route can be split in two at the girdle ledge, but is best enjoyed as one of the finest long pitches in Wales.

45m. Climb steeply to reach a wide crack. Follow this to reach a good resting ledge at 18 metres. Climb direct to the girdle ledge (possible belay) then step right and follow the crack to easier climbing on the arete.

FA. J.Brown, D.Whillans 1951

❻ Ivy Sepulchre 　 E1 5b

A sometimes overlooked classic with good protection and nice moves. Considered easier than *Cenotaph Corner*.

1) 8m. Climb rightwards through vegetated rock to blocks that leads up to the ledge.

2) 5b, 35m. Follow the steep corner, passing a difficult bulge. Can take slightly longer to dry than neighbouring routes.

FA. P.Harding, E.Phillips (2pts) 1947

The south side of The Pass has a set of shadowy and mysterious cliffs, the routes are often long and complex and the rock can take a while to dry. The mountain adventures here are second to none and there are enough routes to keep even the most ardent activist happy for many years.

Approach

The approach is the same as for the cliffs on the north side: 'The Pass' sits southeast of the village of Llanberis, straddling the A4086. Parking is found for the crags in the many laybys up the valley. If these are full it is possible to park in Nant Peris and take the bus up the valley. The crags are usually approached fairly directly from their closest layby via small paths.

Conditions

The south side cliffs are slower to dry and colder than their north side sisters. However, the nose of Dinas Mot takes no seepage and dries rapidly and is also one of the closest of these crags to the road. Get on it! The other crags are generally best left for warmish weather and a good dry spell of a couple of days.

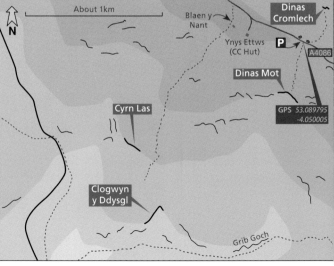

About 1km

N

Blaen y Nant

Dinas Cromlech

Ynys Ettws (CC Hut) P A4086

Dinas Mot

GPS 53.089795
-4.050005

Cyrn Las

Clogwyn y Ddysgl

Grib Goch

Tremadog
Cwm Silyn
Clogwyn
Llanberis
Lliwedd
Ogwen
Carneddau
Betws y Coed
Welsh Winter

Tremadog

Cwm Silyn

Clogwy

Llanberis

Lliwedd

Ogwen

Carneddau

Betws y Coed

Welsh Winter

Omer Shavit climbing *Super Direct* (E1) -
page 97 - on Dinas Mot. Photo: Mark Reeves

Direct Route

The Nose of Dinas Mot is a fast-drying slab of perfect mountain rock and is home to some of the best technical pitches in Wales. Good footwork and small wires help!

Approach - The crag is approached directly from the Cromlech boulder layby via a small track up the hill.

Descent - Getting off The Nose can be tricky, especially in the wet. Abseiling or scrambling down Western Gully (marked) is the norm, but care is required. There is an awkward step at the bottom, which is often wet.

Abseil/scramble descent

3

Lorraine Direct (HVS)

5

2

5

4

1   3

Tremadog · Cwm Silyn · Cloggy · Llanberis · Llilwedd · Ogwen · Carneddau · Betws y Coed · Welsh Winter

1 The Cracks . . . . ☆3 ☐ HS 4c

One of the finest climbs at this grade in the Llanberis Pass. The final pitch sports a tough 4c mantel, though it can be easily avoided if required!

1) 4a, 30m. Pull steeply on the well worn ledge and follow the groove leftwards to ledges. Stride left and climb diagonally leftwards up a thin corner to a short crack. Climb this to belay below an overhang. A sparsely protected pitch.

2) 4a, 10m. Traverse right under the overhang to a chimney. Climb this to a ledge.

3) 4b, 15m. Climb the thin crack in the slab on the left, pass a ledge and step up and walk right to belay on a large pinnacle.

4) 4a, 18m. Surmount the pinnacle and move right onto a ledge. Climb the crack in the left wall of the corner above to another ledge.

5) 4c, 15m. Head up and right to make the slippery mantel onto a rounded ledge (or not!). Move left and climb the wonderful arete to the rock summit.

FA. B.Bathurst, H.Bathurst 1930

2 Lorraine . . . ☆3 🧗 ☐ VS 5a

For those who found *The Cracks* easy enough, *Lorraine* provides a great sister-route.

1) 15m. Follow *The Cracks* to ledges at 12m then belay a little higher.

2) 4c, 15m. Go up leftwards over a bulge to reach a left-slanting groove. Follow this until a step left reaches the short chimney on *The Cracks*.

3) 4c, 15m. Climb the slabby corner crack and a further crack to the pinnacle.

4) 4c, 18m. Surmount the pinnacle and move right onto a ledge. Climb the corner crack to good block belays.

5) 5a, 15m. As for *The Cracks* final pitch.

FA. J.Barford, N.E.Morin 1941.

3 Direct Route . . . ☆3 ☐ VS 5b

One for the well-rounded VS leader.

1) 4a, 15m. Scramble past the twin pinnacles and head up for 10m. Traverse left to belay as for *Lorraine*.

2) 4b, 25m. Go up and right, passing a blunt rib to reach a shallow groove. Climb this to a good belay in a bay.

3) 4c, 15m. Move up right to a diagonal crack. Hand traverse this to a step right onto a large ledge and flake belay.

4) 5b, 18m. The polished corner on the left leads desperately to flake cracks and a corner.

FA. C.Kirkus, J.Dodd 1930

4 Super Direct. ☆3 🧗 ☐ E1 5b

Are you a slab-master or a crack-addict? *Photo on page 95*.

1) 4b, 30m. Start as for *Direct Route*, then, where that route moves left, head down and right and traverse above a rock scar. Move up to belay on a ledge 6m below an overhang.

2) 5b, 30m. One of the best slab pitches in Wales and therefore the world! Climb past the small overhang to a good runner on *Diagonal*. Step up then traverse left to a thin crack. Follow this (technique required) up to the ledge on *Direct Route*.

3) 5b, 15m. Climb the pointed flake and then the overhanging corner crack above.

FA. R.Evans, H.Pasquill 1974

5 Diagonal. . . ☆3 🧗 ☐ HVS 5a

A fantastic and excitingly technical route.

1) 5a, 30m. Start as for *Direct Route* then follow a groove left of the rock scar. Climb the left side of a flake, then traverse right to a good stance under a small overhang.

2) 5a, 15m. Move diagonally right to the chimney and climb it to a small stance.

3) 5a, 20m. Traverse right to a scoop, follow this and go right to a bold mantel onto a ledge. Go up (pocket) to a crack then to a stance.

4) 4c, 15m. The tough corner crack above.

FA. A.Birtwhistle, G.Parkinson 1938

Tremadog
Cwm Silyn
Ogwen
Llanberis
Llŷwedd
Ogwen
Carneddau
Gogarth & North Wales Coast
Welsh Winter

Western Slabs

More good routes on the right-hand side of The Nose including two longer expeditions to the top of the crag.

Descent - Getting off The Nose can be tricky, especially in the wet. Abseiling or scrambling down Western Gully (marked) is the norm, but care is required. There is an awkward step at the bottom, which is often wet.

For the two routes that go to the top, scramble upwards and walk a long way left to reach scree which skirts round and back down to the base of the crag.

① West Rib . . . . . .   HVS 5a

Another classic HVS, supposedly slightly easier than the neighbouring *Diagonal*.

1) 4b, 18m. Start 4m left of the wall. Climb up a chimney then move leftwards to belay left of the obvious rib.

2) 5a, 30m. Traverse right to the rib, climb it to a high step at 9m (good runner) and weave delicately up to join *Western Slabs*.

3) 4c, 18m. Move round the arete on the left and climb a thin crack. Pass the steep arete and go right to meet *Western Slabs*.

FA. C.Kirkus, I.Waller 1931

② Western Slabs . .   VS 4c

A good route with nice positions.

1) 4b, 15m. From just left of the wall, step onto the quartzy block to gain and follow a groove on the right. The ledge above is reached by stepping round the arete, belay.

2) 4b, 22m. Climb to the lower of two small overlaps, pass this on the right, step right and climb over to the second overlap. Follow a groove to a ledge, then continue rightwards up another groove to another ledge.

3) 4c, 25m. Step down and left and follow the groove to a ledge by a large flake. Climb the groove on the right. Finish leftwards.

FA. J.M.Edwards, A.Edge, A.D'Aeth 1931

③ Slow Ledge Climb   VS 4b

A superb way to continue your adventure.

1) 15m. Scramble up and right towards the quartzy pinnacle above the descent gully. Move right just below the top of the pinnacle onto heather, move diagonally right to a short groove and a ledge. Continue zigzagging rightwards with care to reach a tree and flake belay. Beware of people below.

2) 4b, 25m. Move right and up to a large flake. Climb the rightward trending slab to gain a hand traverse which leads to the 'Slow Ledge'. From the right side of the ledge climb a groove then make another hand traverse right to gain a heathery belay.

3) 4a, 25m. Climb directly up into an unappealing groove and move left round a rib into another groove. Weave upwards on easier ground to a ledge.

4) 25m. Scramble off and belay well back.

FA. J.M.Edwards, J.Gask 1934

Evening | 20 min

Descent

3

1

2

4

④ Black Spring . . . ☆2 ☐ HVS 5a

A good, but tough climb with technical moves and an often wet second pitch. Start by scrambling up to the terrace.

1) 5a, 25m. Follow the crack for 10m. Move left for 3m and follows pockets to a steepening. Pass this and move left to a cave.

2) 5a, 32m. Pass the overlap on the right and gain a steep slab on the right.

Follow a shallow groove, then break left to a quartzy groove which leads to a large ledge.

3) 4a, 15m. Climb up broken ground to meet *Slow Ledge Climb* at the flake.

4) 4c, 35m. Follow a crack on the left to a large roof. Traverse rightwards to belay at a junction with *Slow Ledge Climb*.

5) 40m. Slabby climbing leads to the top.

FA. M.Boysen, A.Williams 1965

Plexus

The rough, slabby rock of the Plexus Buttress is the Welsh answer to gritstone. Bring that slab technique!

Approach - The buttress lies to the right of the main crag of Dinas Mot. See page 94.

Descent - A long single abseil gets you to the base of the crag.

A

2

3

1

Alternative 5a start

1

Approach

❶ **Plexus**. . . . . 🔲 E1 5b

Both technical and adventurous, the classic of the buttress is a superb route and, since the demise of the ancient peg, is now a slightly bolder affair.

1) 20m. Climb easily up a short groove to the large ledge. Follow the ledge leftwards and move up to a stance under the clean groove. There is an alternative direct start at **5a**.

2) 5a, 20m. Follow the groove above to a bulge, pull over this and step right onto the clean slab. Climb the crack on the left until a traverse leftwards to the arete is possible. Continue to a good belay.

3) 5b, 25m. Move up and right to the weakest part of the capping roof. Turn the beefy roof and balance leftward into the corner. Move up, then traverse right onto a technical slab and continue to a ledge and perched block. Pass the block to gain a scoop, leave the scoop on its right side and continue diagonally left to a good stance.

4) 4b, 15m. Follow the line of least resistance up the final slabs.

FA. J.Ingle, P.Crew (2pts) 1962

❷ **Ten Degrees North** . . . . 🔲 E2 5c

Simply the best crux sequence in the Llanberis Pass. Were you bamboozled?

1) 20m. As for *Plexus* pitch 1.

2) 5b, 10m. Climb a wall then head right (peg) to the groove. Follow this to reach technical moves to enter the scoop on the left. Belay on the slab.

3) 5c, 20m. Smear, palm and contort up the rounded groove to reach a small roof. Pass this on the right and climb up to a peg, then head to a small overhang and trend up and right to a good belay just right of the huge capping roof.

4) 5b, 10m. Move left and climb the flake to reach a traverse line leading left round the arete to join *Plexus* and belay at the perched block on pitch 3.

5) 4b, 20m. Climb the rest of pitch 3 and then pitch 4 of *Plexus* in one pitch.

FA. A.Sharp, J.Zangwill 1974

❸ **Nexus** . . . . 🔲 E1 5b

Perhaps the best out of the three routes, *Nexus* is an absolute classic and is a good stern test for any aspiring E1 leader. The rock is superb throughout.

1) 6m. Start as for *Plexus*, but belay on the first large ledge.

2) 5b, 30m. A long, sustained and superb pitch. Follow the slab just right of the large corner to the roof. Hand traverse leftwards under the roof to the arete (thread). Pull round the roof via the good layback-crack and gain the diagonal ramp. Follow this up and right to gain a sloping ledge on the right. Follow the short crack to a shallow groove leading to a good stance just right of the huge roof (junction with *Ten Degrees North*).

3) 4b, 12m. Climb the slab on the right until the angle steepens, then move left onto a ledge. Traverse left along a horizontal break (tricky) to a swing round the arete. Belay in the scoop.

4) 4b, 20m. Climb the rest of pitch 3 and then pitch 4 of *Plexus* in one pitch.

FA. M.Boysen, P.Nunn (1pt) 1963

The Gambit Climb

The left side of this mountain crag is home to many classic adventures.

Approach - Follow the path marked on the map on page 94 past Cyrn Las.

Descent - Either descend *Western Gully* or continue up the scramble of *Clogwyn y Person Arete*.

Clogwyn y Person Arete - a classic ridge scramble

Descent scramble down the ridge and down Western Gully

The Parson's Nose and Western Gully to its right

2

3

Tremadog

Cwm Silyn

Ogwen

Llanberis

Lliwedd

Ogwen

Carneddau

Ysbyty y Gwryd

Welsh Winter

❶ The Parson's Nose . . . . ▢ Diff

This classic route (not shown) tackles the front of the nose of rock via a series of pleasant pitches. The route lies at the lowest point of the rock nose, down and left of the main crag.
1) 25m. Climb directly up the low-angled slabs of clean rock.
2) 20m. Continue up the slab as it steepens, then trend diagonally right to a stance at the base of a shallow groove.
3) 15m. Climb diagonally rightwards, following a faint crackline, to reach a large ledge above the gully on the right.
4) 15m. Easy ground leads to the summit of the nose. A descent can be made down the gully on the right (*Western Gully*), or scramble along the ridge of *Clogwyn y Person Arete*.
FA. A.Stocker 1884!

❷ The Gambit Climb. . . . . ▢ VDiff

One of the finest mountain VDiffs in the UK, *The Gambit Climb* has it all. Acres of exposure, superb moves, great rock and a crux at the end. What more could you ask for? The start of the route lies 5m left of a unique pocketed wall, around 60m right of *Western Gully*.
1) 23m. Climb a crack past a hanging flake for 3m and then move left. Move down and left to gain a slab at its left edge. Follow this slab to a corner-crack. Climb this to gain a ledge, then follow a continuation crack above to reach large ledges.
2) 17m. The line of least resistance leads up via a chimney to reach a large grassy ledge known as The Green Collar.
3) 15m. Traverse right to gain a short chimney. Climb this to the next ledge.
4) 15m. Move left along the ledge to the base of a chimney. Follow this to gain the top of the pinnacle on the left. Step right and follow the crack above to more ledges.
5) 15m. Above is a rightward sloping ledge that is followed to a square-cut corner. Climb this with difficulty via a thin crack to gain easy ground.
FA. J.Thompson, H.Jones, K.Orton 1910

❸ The Ring . . . . ▢ VS 4c

A steep and sometimes technical route that weaves its way up the cliff via lines of weakness and chimneys. The route starts half way between *The Gambit Climb* and *Fallen Block Crack* (on the following page) at a steep groove 3m right of some vague chimney lines.
1) 4a, 15m. Climb the groove past its undercut base and then move left round a corner. Head up 10m to gain some large perched blocks and continue up to a stance 5m above.
2) 12m. Move up and wander left to a grass-filled corner system. Follow this, passing 3 large steps, to reach a belay in the next corner system above.
3) 4b, 15m. Climb the corner, stepping left onto a ledge at 5m. Climb the technical wall above, then traverse right to belay by a small slab.
4) 4c, 15m. Gain a small, crimpy hold on the left which unlocks the secret of the slab, allowing access to its far edge. Follow a chimney, then a crack to belay at a perched block.
5) 20m. Move left and follow a cracked corner to gain the right end of a ledge. Move left a few metres to gain a short wall then a slab which leads to a ledge below a corner.
6) 4b, 40m. Climb the left-hand of the two corner cracks to a ledge at 5m. Follow the corner on the right via steep jamming. Continue up easy ground above.
FA. P.Harding, J.Disley 1948

1 Fallen Block Crack .... ☆2 🧗 ☐ VS 4c

A good, wide, traditional crack, for good, wide, traditional climbers! Start at the fallen block.
1) 4a, 10m. Follow the short, strenuous crack to belay at a chockstone.
2) 4c, 25m. Follow the steep crack above to gain a rest at 10m. Continue straight up the slightly relenting fissure to reach *The Black Gates*.
3) 40m. Follow pitches 4 and 5 of *The Black Gates*.
FA. I.Waller 1927

2 Route of Knobs .... ☆1 🧗 ☐ HVS 5a

Another fine exposed mountain-route with a technical second pitch.
1) 4a, 10m. *Fallen Block Crack* pitch 1.
2) 5a, 30m. A hold on the right wall gives access to the arete. Climb this for 5m to a ledge then traverse right, passing a thin crack to reach a groove. Climb the groove then move back to the middle of the wall. Trend right to gain a crack leading to a ledge on *Fallen Block Crack*.
3) 4b, 12m. Traverse left to climb the left wall.
4) 30m. Follow the remaining sections of pitches 4 and 5 of *The Black Gates*.
FA. J.M.Edwards, H.Bryson 1952

3 The Black Gates .... ☆1 🧗 ☐ VDiff

A great and often forgotten route that takes in some superb settings with some strenuous climbing. Start 15m right of the fallen block at a faint groove, down and right of the pinnacles.
1) 10m. Climb the groove for 10m to reach a stance below large boulders.
2) 35m. Surmount the boulders to gain a niche below a towering pinnacle. Struggle out of the niche and follow a crack to the top of the pinnacle on the left. Continue for 5m, then belay.
3) 12m. Follow the corner for 3m and make a breath-taking step round the corner to reach a ledge on the left. Climb the wall, pass a ledge and continue to a second ledge to belay.
4) 10m. Move to the left edge of the ledge and climb the chimney for 6m. Head right and up for 10m over easy ground to reach another chimney.
5) 20m. Climb the traditional chimney, complete with chockstone, to gain a ledge on the right. Finish up the slab via the corner crack at the left end.
FA. G.Mallory 1915

4 Rectory Chimneys .... ☆2 ☐ VDiff

A classic of the Llanberis Pass, one of the best routes at the VDiff grade. Start 25m right of the fallen block at a narrow chimney with a flake leaning across it at half height.
1) 18m. Ascend the chimney making good use of the flake. Follow a groove up a steep wall.
2) 20m. Climb the short, steep wall on the left, then follow the short crack to mantel into a niche. Step left and enter the crack above from behind. Follow this to a stance 5m above.
3) 12m. Climb into the corner above and traverse left along the ledge to a chimney. Climb the chimney to a ledge and good belay.
4) 20m. Easy, broken ground leads to a large grassy rake.
5) 40m. Follow the grassy rake rightwards to reach a large jumble of rocks; The Vestry.
6) 25m. Traverse to the chimney 6m to the right. Climb easily up this.
FA. M.Guiness, W.McNaught, H.Carr 1925

Descent scramble down the ridge and down Western Gully

Rectory Chimneys
The right side of Clogwyn y Ddysgl has a bunch of long classic mountain routes with great climbing on good rock.
Approach - Follow the path marked on the map on page 94 past Cyrn Las.
Descent - Either descend *Western Gully* or continue up the scramble of *Clogwyn y Person Arete.*

Evening 60 min

Tremadog

Cwm Silyn

Cloggy

Llanberis

Lliwedd

Ogwen

Carneddau

Betws y Coed

Welsh Winter

1

2

3

4

Cyrn Las

Cyrn Las is a high mountain crag with a big feel. Grassy slopes need to be negotiated to reach the base of all routes.
Approach - Follow the path from the farm. See page 94.
Descent - Head left to reach the main path down the hillside.

Descent

Overhanging Arete (E2)

① Main Wall . . . 🕭🗺️ ☐ HS 4b

One of the classic, must-do routes of the UK, but not a route to be underestimated. Scramble up rightwards to below and left of a triangular overhang which is below a grassy terrace.

1) 4a, 20m. Follow the well-travelled slab up and left to a ledge at 10m. Climb a short corner for 3m and move right across a slab, round a rib and up to a stance on a pulpit.

2) 4b, 25m. Follow the tricky rightward-leaning gangway on the right to reach *Subsidiary Grooves*. Follow this for a few metres, then traverse left on a ledge to reach a corner and blunt arete overlooking the large gully. Gear at foot level for the belay.

3) 4a, 15m. Climb the blunt arete and move diagonally right to a triangular ledge in a corner.

4) 4b, 25m. The big pitch! Drop down a little way, then climb up the pinnacle on the left. From the top of the pinnacle, step left onto the steep wall. Pull up into a niche and head round the corner on the left to gain a steep arete. Follow this until it is possible to step across the chimney and gain a short slab.

5) 4a, 25m. Move up to an overhang, then step across left, passing a broken chimney to gain the base of a large slab that overlooks the large gully. Climb the exposed left edge of the slab on good holds to a stance.

6) 30m. Climb leftwards to a ledge, follow the slab on the right, scramble up easy ground to finish.

FA. P.Roberts, J.Cooke 1935

② Subsidiary Grooves

. . . . 🕭🗡️▨ ☐ E1 5b

A good route with a tough final-pitch.

1) 4a, 26m. Follow *Main Wall* to the first stance, then move across to belay at the base of the chimney/groove on the right.

2) 4b, 15m. Climb the groove to meet *Main Wall* then step right to belay.

3) 5a, 40m. Climb a crack above, on dodgy rock, to another junction with *Main Wall*.

Make a diagonal traverse left for 6m up a steep wall, then head back right up a gangway to a rest in a corner. Climb the steep wall above.

4) 4c, 15m. Climb the groove to the overhang. Teeter over poor rock on the right to gain a corner, then romp up the easy slab on the right to a good stance and belay.

5) 5b, 15m. This short tough pitch follows the easy crack on the left of the slab to the steep corner. Climb this (crux). Scramble off.

FA. J.Brown, D.Whillans 1953

③ Lubyanka . . . 🕭🗺️ ☐ E3 5c

A fantastically bold and exposed route with some technical climbing and a grand finale.

1 and 2) 4b, 45m. As for *Main Wall*.

3) 5c, 18m. Climb the groove above the stance, enter from the left to belay in a bay.

4) 5b, 15m. Follow the corner behind the bay, exit right and go down to a spike belay.

5) 5c, 20m. Go directly up the slab, pass an overlap to gain a short corner. Climb this to a tricky exit left onto a short slab and a ledge.

6) 5c, 22m. Rail rightwards along the break above the void and make a tough move to get stood up just left of the arete. Climb the groove above past a roof onto easier ground.

FA. E.Cleasby, J.Eastham, R.Matheson 1976

Approach The Grooves via grassy terraces.

④ The Grooves. . . . 🕭 ☐ E1 5b

Simply the best E1 in Wales?

1) 5b, 45m. Climb easily up to the roof then gain the groove. Follow this to a ledge then climb the wall above and left to a large ledge.

2) 5b, 40m. Follow the continuation groove above to a ledge. A wall leads to another ledge.

3) 5b, 35m. Gain a left slanting ledge above and traverse left to the second groove. Follow this to gain easier ground leading to the top.

FA. J.Brown, D.Cowans, E.Price 1953

The steep arete to the right of the final pitch of The Grooves is **Overhanging Arete***, a superb 3-star pitch of* **E2 5b***.*

Tremadog
Cwm Silyn
Clogwy
Llanberis
Lliwedd
Ogwen
Carneddau
Betws y Coed
Winter

Lliwedd

The long, rambling nature of Lliwedd means that it is possible to climb almost anywhere and the route descriptions and lines are easy to misinterpret as the whole easy angled cliff is covered in grooves, features and ledges. Go, climb up, and have fun! Lliwedd isn't about chasing grades, it's about reaching the summit, soaking up the view and heading back to the Vaynol for a good pint of Robinson's.

Approach

The approach for Lliwedd takes you up into the highest mountains of Snowdonia, and the summit of the crag is a great view point and from there many teams continue up to the top of Snowdon. Park at Pen y Pass car park at the top of the Llanberis Pass (or get the park and ride bus from Nant Peris). Follow the Miners track to Llyn Llydaw, the large lake, where the main track goes to the right of the lake, follow the left side of the lake and then make a break up the steep hillside direct to the base of the crag.

For Clowyn y Wenallt see page 114

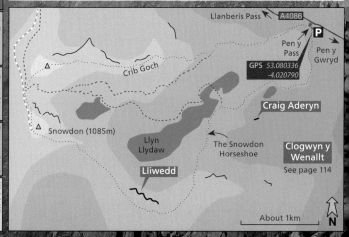

Tremadog

Cwm Silyn

Clogwyn

Llanberis

Lliwedd

Ogwen

Carneddau

Betws y Coed

Welsh Winter

Conditions

Lliwedd takes a lot of drainage, is very high up in the mountains and only gets early morning sun. The routes take a couple of days to dry out; and due to the nature of the rock, wet ascents are not really recommended. As with all high crags, warm clothes are essential.

Ed Douglas on *Longland's Continuation* (S) - *page 111* - on Lliwedd. Photo: Ray Wood

Terminal Arete

Descent

East Gully

Great Terrace

Terminator - next page

Birch Tree Terrace

Heather Shelf

1

2

3

Avalanche

Approach - From the Pen y Pass car park, follow the Miner's Track to the lake. Then take the path leading leftwards, which leads to the scree slopes at the foot of the buttress.

Descent - Walk towards the top of the pass until it is possible to make a steep descent of a wide grass-gully. NOT East Gully.

Tremadog
Cwm Silyn
Cloggy
Llanberis
Lliwedd
Ogwen
Carneddau
Betws-y-Coed
Welsh Winter

Early morning
60 min

❶ Horned Crag Route ⚐ ☐ VDiff

One of the first routes climbed on the cliff, and a real mountaineering adventure. Start on the far left of Heather Shelf.

1) 20m. Climb up blocky terrain and traverse leftwards to belay beneath the big corner.
2) 27m. Climb the corner until it is possible to step left onto the prow. Follow this to a vegetated ledge.
3) 30m. Climb the broader rib above to another, larger heather-ledge.
4) 30m. Climb the wall to reach the vague chimney on its right-hand side. Ascend this, and follow a quartz band rightwards to a ledge.
5) 23m. Scramble up to belay on the left end of the grassy ledge, beneath the Horns.
6) 20m. The groove above leads to another, steeper groove. Climb this until a move rightwards leads to the base of the slab below the horns.
7) 8m. Climb the slab. From here 100m of exposed scrambling leads to the summit.
FA. J.Thompson, O.Eckenstein 1905

❷ Paradise . . . . . . ⚐ ☐ HS 4a

A sustained outing leading to the classic scramble of *Terminal Arete*.

1) 4a, 30m. Follow the groove, forking right at its juction to reach a ledge. A quartz band on the right leads to a stance below a grass ledge.
2) 4a, 23m. A short groove up and left bypasses an overhang. Climb to the ledge above and belay below a prominent V-groove.
3) 4a, 25m. Step out leftwards and climb the slab until moves back right lead to another ledge above the last belay.
4) 30m. Traverse rightwards to a the arete of a quartzy wall. Climb up this to to a stance level with the grassy ledge on the left.
5) 30m. Follow the arete to a spike belay.
6) 35m. Easy climbing leads up and left-wards to a stance above the left-hand tip of the Great Terrace.
7) and 8) 120m. From here the classic finish **Terminal Arete (D)** leads to the summit.
FA. H.Jones, R.Backwell 1909

❸ Avalanche/Red Wall/
Longland's Continuation ⚐ ☐ S 4b

A route that is steeped in history, and the classic of the buttress. Start below the right-hand end of Heather Shelf. *Photo on page 109.*

1) 20m. Follow the groove to Heather Shelf.
2) 30m. Climb diagonally rightwards onto a face, then climb upwards to belay 4m left of a prominent spike, level with a dog-leg in the corner off to the right.
3) 15m. Climb up to belay left of a quartz band.
4) 25m. Move right and climb the quartz band. The groove above leads to moves rightwards to gain some ledges. Move onto the right-hand side of the rib to the right and climb it to a spike belay.
5) 33m. A vegetated groove up and right leads to a tall, thin block.
6) 33m. A scramble rightwards along a shelf leads to a stance on the Great Terrace.
7) 4a, 24m. (The start of **Red Wall**). Move rightwards to a grassy groove. Climb this to a hard move onto a rib leading to some good ledges. Belay at the bottom of a deep groove pointing towards the top of **Terminal Arete**.
8) 4a, 30m. Climb up a rib, passing a pin-nacle on the right to a ledge. Climb the short wall to the Green Gallery.
9) 10m. Climb leftwards to belay about 10m left of the huge gully.
10) 25m. (The start of **Longland's Continuation**) Climb the left arete of a steep face to a hollow. A jammed block leads rightwards to a slab. Climb the slab, trending rightwards after 6m and pass another slab to belay in a grassy slot.
11) 30m. Follow a rib on the right to belay beneath a steep slab.
12) 4b, 15m. The final pitch is the crux slab! It can be climbed direct, or trend left at half height.
FA. J.Thompson, E.Reynolds 1907
FA. (Longland's) J.Longland 1929

Early morning | 60 min

← Descent

Terminal Arete

Great Terrace

Avalanche Red Wall - previous page

Birch Tree Terrace

Tremadog · Cwm Silyn · Cloggy · Llanberis · Lliwedd · Ogwen · Carneddau · Betws y Coed · Welsh Winter

❶ Terminator · · 🌟🎦☐ E1 5b

The modern route up the buttress. Start at a rib leading up the left-hand side of the face beneath Birch Tree Terrace.

1) 5a, 30m. Climb the rib (bold) to Birch Tree Terrace. Belay beneath a steep groove.

2) 5b, 50m. Climb onto the slab via a block on the right. Climb straight up to reach a belay in some quartzy niches.

3) 5a, 25m. An overhanging groove leads to easier climbing. Follow the grain of the cliff to belay at the base of a corner/groove.

4) 35m. Climb past the groove on its left and belay at the prominent square block.

5) 5b, 35m. weave your way up the wall above, trending into the left-hand groove. Follow it for around 18m to a grassy ledge with a large block. Mount the block and climb the wall behind to the base of **Terminal Arete**.

7) and 8) 120m. Follow **Terminal Arete (D)** to the summit.

FA. J.Hope, K.Neal 1990

❷ The Sword/Route 2 🌟☐ VS 4c

A fine, open route leading to Great Terrace, from where a choice of finishes is available. After a hard first pitch, the rest is only VDiff.

1) 4c, 50m. Climb the corner to an overlap, then move leftwards to a ledge. Climb the rib above directly, past 'the Quartz Babe' to belay 5m after the Babe's tip.

2) 20m. Continue easily to a bollard belay.

3) 14m. Climb up and right from the top of the tallest block to some big holds, then move easily back left to belay on a ledge beneath a groove.

4) 40m. Follow the groove, passing a possible belay at 12m, before moving right into another groove that leads, eventually, to a small ledge.

5) 30m. Easy climbing leads to the Great Terrace. From here, pick a finish up **Terminal Arete**, or *Avalanche/Red Wall*.

FA. (The Sword) J.Edwards, J.Buzzard, F.Champion 1938. FA. (Route 2) J.Thopmson, O.Eckstein 1904

3 Jacob's Media . . . ⭐ HS 4a
A fine slab pitch linking two existing routes to give the best climb on the crag.
50m. Start 5m left of the arete and climb directly up to quartzy pockets. Head slightly right, then at half height move back left and follow a crack to the very tip of the slab.
FA. (As Via Media) F.Graham, M.Guinness 1925

4 Arete Climb . . . . ⭐ Diff
An enjoyable outing up the right arete.
50m. Follow the arete, passing a possible belay at 30m.
FA. S.W.Herford 1913

5 Subsidiary Slab . ⭐ Mod
The easiest route in the book. A pleasant scramble up the smaller set-back slab. A belay is possible at the top of the first slab.

sh Tree Rib (Diff)

Descent

Jacob's Media
A high but fast-drying slab, ideal for those wanting to get away from it all.
Approach - Follow the Miners Track to Llyn Teyrn. Break left down the hill to cross the large pipe line. Continue across marshy ground (30 mins total).
Descent - Head well right from the top of the crag and descend the ridge.

Tremadog
Cwm Silyn
Cloggy
Llanberis
Lliwedd
Ogwen
Carneddau
Bettws y Coed
Welsh Winter

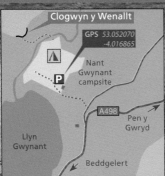

Clogwyn y Wenallt

GPS 53.052070
-4.016865

Nant Gwynant campsite

A498

Pen y Gwryd

Llyn Gwynant

Beddgelert

Approach - The crag halfway down the Gwynant valley, at the head of Llyn Gwynant. From Pen y Pass, head away from Llanberis and turn right at the T junction. At the bottom of the hill lies the big lake (Llyn Gwynant) and a superb campsite on your right. Park at the campsite, go to the back corner and cross a small bridge over the river. Turn left and follow the path downstream for 100m until a vague track heads steeply up to the base of the cliff on your right.

① Ferdinand 〉 E2 5b

A classic Joe Brown jamming-crack. Steep, powerful and intimidating, brill!
10m. Wander a little higher up the hillside to the left of the crag and walk along a good ledge to a flat spot beneath the steep corner and crack. Leave the ledge via a boulder problem and climb the corner for a few metres until a hard move right gains the crack. Let the battle commence!
FA. J.Brown, C.Jones 1959

② Oxine 〉 VS 4c

A great combination of the first pitch of a VS called *Oxo* and the steep and thrilling top pitch of *Bovine*.
1) 4b, 30m. Start 10m left of the wall that touches the crag. Climb up a few metres and traverse right to a small ledge. Continue rightwards, passing a pinnacle to reach a small flat wall, pass this and gain the ledge on the right. Good belay.
2) 4c, 28m. This is what you came for. Steep, exposed climbing on holds the size of the Starship Entreprise. Climb the groove above the ledge for 2m, make a hard move right to huge holds and blast-off directly up the wall.
FA. (1st pitch) J.Lees, G.Roberts, W.Trench 1953
FA. C.Davies, B.Wright, D.McKelvey 1957

③ Bovero 〉 E2 5b

1) 5a, 28m. Start beneath a groove 5m left of the stone wall, midway between *Oxine* and the wall. Climb the wall to the pinnacle on *Oxine*, blast up the groove above to the good ledge on the left.
2) 5b, 30m. Boulder off the ledge on to the flake above and gain a scoop. Step right to a flake, and continue to easier ground. Hop left in to the groove and climb this to the top.
FA. J.Brown, D.Whillans (1pt) 1959

④ The Poacher 〉 E5 6b

One for the hard boys and girls.
1) 5a, 28m. As for *Bovero*.
2) 5c, 15m. From the right-hand end of the ledge, climb a groove to an awkward stance.
3) 6b, 15m. The bulging wall above leads past a peg to a groove and the top.
FA. P.Burke, G.Kent (1pt) 1978. FFA. R.Fawcett 1980

⑤ The Death Wisher 〉 E2 5b

A great, harder alternative to *Oxine*.
1) 4b, 30m. As for *Oxine*.
2) 5b, 26m. Climb the groove as for *Oxine* and where that route moves right, break left to a thin, precarious flake. Follow this to gain cracks which are climbed to the top.
FA. M.Crook, S.McCartney 1977

Tremadog

Cwm Silyn

Cloggy

Llanberis

Lliwedd

Ogwen

Carneddau

Betws y Coed

Welsh Winter

Descent

Clogwyn y Wenallt

Clogwyn y Wenallt is a low-lying valley crag with pristine rock, a beautiful open aspect and gorgeous views over the lake. You can get pumped on the top pitch of *Oxine* and cool off by taking a dip in the lake!

Conditions - Clogwyn y Wenallt gets morning sun and dries quickly. It can be very warm in summer and can also get a few midges as it lies close to the lake.

Descent - Walk off to the left and follow a small path back to the base of the crag.

 Ogwen

Tremadog

Cwm Silyn

Clogwyn

Llanberis

Lliwedd

Ogwen

Carneddau

Betws-y-Coed

Welsh Winter

Tremadog

Cwm Silyn

Cloggy

Llanberis

Lliwedd

Ogwen

Carneddau

Betws y Coed

Welsh Winter

Sophie Evitt on pitch 4 of *Gashed Crag* (VDiff) -
page 123 - Tryfan East Face. Photo: Jack Geldard

Tremadog

Cwm Silyn

Cloggy

Llanberis

Lliwedd

Ogwen

Carneddau

Betws y Coed

Welsh Winter

The Ogwen valley is a major climbing destination, with hillsides covered in huge sweeps of perfect rock, of all grades and angles. Due to the excellent climbing, the Ogwen valley can get quite busy. The Idwal slabs, Little Tryfan and Milestone buttress are all very popular, and for good reason. To escape the crowds a trip up to the magnificent Glyder Fach is well worth the walk. We are particularly proud of our pages on Little Tryfan, a crag that hasn't seen much attention from guidebook writers in the past, but has seen a lot of attention from climbers. This clean slab of rock is an ideal place to take your first steps on rock, or to hone your skills ready for the challenges of the bigger cliffs.

Conditions

Some of the higher, north-facing cliffs such as Glyder Fach and the Idwal Slabs can take a few days to dry out completely, but the positive nature of the holds and the plentiful runners (especially on the Idwal Slabs) mean that ascents can be made (and are made) in damp conditions. However, in the depths of winter it might be a wise idea to look elsewhere – Tremadog maybe? The lower lying crags of the Ogwen valley, such as Milestone Buttress, dry a little faster and see ascents for much of the year.

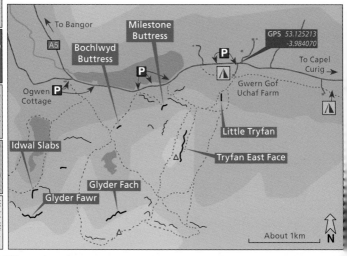

Approach

The Ogwen valley lies next to the A5, just south of the village of Bethesda. The crags in this chapter mainly lie on the south west side of the road, and are approached from the free parking laybys or the campsite parking, as described on each individual crag page.

Tremadog

Cwm Silyn

Cloggy

Llanberis

Lliwedd

Ogwen

Carneddau

Betws y Coed

Welsh Winter

Rachael Barlow on *Sub Cneifion Rib* (VDiff) - *page 138* - in Cwm Idwal. Photo: Jack Geldard.

Tremadog | Cwm Silyn | Cloggy | Llanberis | Lliwedd | **Ogwen** | Carneddau | Betws y Coed | Welsh Winter

❶ Little Tryfan Arete   Diff
A classic scramble/climb up the left arete.
1) 26m. Large holds lead to the ridge which is followed to a comfortable belay.
2) 26m. The ridge is followed to the top.

❷ Crack 1 . . . .   Mod
The wide crack has good gear and stances.
1) 25m. A line of flakes and cracks leads to a good niche-belay.
2) 12m. Follow the crack right of the arete.
3) 12m. Continue in the same line to the top.

❸ Crack 2 . . . .   Diff
A popular and well protected route.
1) 38m. A diagonal crack leads to the large triangular niche. Follow the wide crack above to a small, square belay-stance.
2) 12m. As for the previous route.

❹ Crack 3 . . . .   Diff
The hardest of the three crack routes.
1) 25m. Diagonal flakes gain the straight crack. Follow this to a small belay stance.
2) 27m. Follow the right-hand crack to the ledge.

❺ Slab 1 . . . .   VDiff
Start beneath the white "boil" at 23m.
1) 25m. Climb cracks then the slab past the left side of the boil to belay as for *Crack 3*.
2) 27m. Take the left of the two cracks above to rejoin *Crack 3* near the top.

❻ Slab 2 . . . . .   S 4a
A great route up the blank looking slab.
1) 4a, 28m. Head almost directly up the slab past the right side of the boil.
2) 4a, 23m. Continue up the slab above on fine incut holds.

7 Crack 4 .... ☆ □ **Diff**

The wide ragged-crack gives a fine pitch.
1) 30m. Follow the wide crack past a large flake to a good belay on the slab.
2) 20m. Either climb rightwards to the chimney or go direct to the ledge.

Tryfan Fach

A superb sweep of clean rock at an amenable angle, Tryfan Fach is deservedly popular. The face is littered with holds and gear placements making it possible to climb almost anywhere on it below a HS standard.

Descent

Afternoon | 10 min

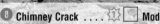

8 Chimney Crack .... ☆ □ **Mod**

The wide chimney likes big boots!
1) 25m. Follow the wide chimney (large gear) to belay above the niche.
2) 20m. Continue easily to the ledge.

10 Stepped Crack .... ☆ □ **Diff**

Start just right of the large gash.
1) 30m. A long and delightful pitch 5m right of the arete to a belay above the heather.
2) 16m. Climb easily to the top.

9 Central Slab Route .. ☆ □ **Diff**

A direct line up the clean slab.
1) 32m. Large holds lead to the centre of the slab. Trend left to belay.
2) 10m. Follow the diagonal crack.

11 Mossy Slab .... □ **HVD**

A pleasantly mossy slab.
1) 30m. Climb directly up the slab to belay by the large heather patch.
2) 17m. Head up and right to the top.

121

Tremadog
Cwm Silyn
Cloggy
Llanberis
Lliwedd
Ogwen
Carreddau
Welsh Winter

Pinnacle Rib Route

The left side of the East face of Tryfan is home to many long and historical routes.
Approach - All routes are approached from the Heather Terrace, a long ledge with a good path that runs along the base of the cliffs. Heather Terrace is reached by continuing up the path from Little Tryfan past a col, then continuing rightwards up steeper ground and then onto the terrace itself. (See map on page 118).
Descent - The easiest descent from the summit of the mountain is via the South Ridge. It is also possible to scramble down North Gully then Little Gully (shown on next page).

To the South Ridge

Thompson's Chimney

Easier finish

2

South Gully (a scramble)

1

3

Heather Terrace

4

Morning   30 min

Tremadog
Cwm Silyn
Clogwyn
Llanberis
Lliwedd
Ogwen
Carneddau
Bettws y Coed
Welsh Winter

1 Gashed Crag . . . 🔲 VDiff

A great, long route up the striking ridge passing the overhang of 'the gash'.
Photo on page 117.

1) 45m. Start 20m left of South Gully, just above a widening in the terrace. Follow a small groove to an overlap at 9m. Turn this rightwards and climb easier ground up and right to ledges beneath the ridge proper.

2) 18m. Follow the ribbed wall up to the large sloping ledge beneath the chimney. Belay on the far right beneath the chimney.

3) 20m. Follow the awkward chimney and climb the wall above leftwards to the ridge.

4) 38m. Follow the exposed and rough ridge (various belays possible).

5) 38m. Continue up the ridge to reach a good ledge below the final tower.

6) 17m. Climb the groove past a tricky roof.
FA. H.Buckle, G.Barlow 1902

The next route starts high up South Gully.

2 Munich Climb . . 🔲 VS 5a

An adventurous mountain route high on the side wall of South Gully. The route is gained by scrambling up South Gully to reach a large grassy ledge to the left of a low rib.

1) 4c, 30m. From the ledge, step down and follow the rightmost groove to reach a steep narrow slab (possible belay). Climb the slab to a hard move to reach the right-hand edge. Belay with care.

2) 5a, 18m. From the right-hand block, boldly gain the nose on the left. Continue left to gain 'Teufel's Crack'. Follow this to a belay on a grassy rake.

3) 15m. Easily up the rake to belay behind the large block.

4) 4b, 38m. Climb a vague groove right of the block. Move left to a crack and follow this to a ledge. Gain a steep crack on the right to reach the top.
FA. H.Teufel, H.Sedlmayr, J.Jenkins (2pts) 1936

3 Overlapping Ridge Route

. . . . 🔲 VDiff

One of Wales' most classic routes. Also known as First Pinnacle Rib. A wonderful, direct voyage up the ridge. The Yellow Slab on pitch 4 has a short 4b technical crux, but it can be skirted round to the right.

1) 10m. Start 10m right of South Gully ("FPR" is scratched on the rock) where a square block leans against the crag. Climb a slab underneath steep rock, exit right. Climb a groove on the right to belay on the ridge.

2) 40m. Follow the easy ridge direct.

3) 40m. Continue up the ridge to the pinnacle. Belay behind the pinnacle.

4) 4b, 15m. The infamous Yellow Slab! Climb the polished slab to a groove on the right. Follow this to a stance. You can avoid this pitch on the right if needed.

5) 35m. Follow the curving rib to easier ground and a belay beneath the final wall.

6) 25m. Either walk rightwards for 20m, belay, then climb straight up **Thompson's Chimney (S)** or head right and take an alternative route onto easier ground.
FA. E.Steeple, G.Barlow, A.Doughty 1914

4 Pinnacle Rib Route

. . . . 🔲 VDiff

Another classic outing up the long ridge 40m right of South Gully. Often called Second Pinnacle Rib ("FPR" is scratched on the rock here too!).

1) 25m. Climb a groove just right of the rib that marks the right-hand side of the large grassy bay to belay on blocks.

2) 30m. Climb the steep rib above.

3) 30m. Climb rock steps to a large stance.

4) 4b, 12m. Continue up the rounded arete above, then traverse left to a stance above the Yellow Slab on the previous route.

5) 35m. As for the previous route.

6) 25m. As for the previous route.
FA. J.Thompson, H.Hughes 1894

Grooved Arete

Grooved Arete is one of Britain's most famous climbs, and justifiably so. It weaves a remarkable adventure up the huge leaning North-Buttress of Tryfan.

Approach - All routes are approached from the Heather Terrace, a long ledge with a good path that runs along the base of the cliffs. Heather Terrace is reached by continuing up the path from Little Tryfan past a col, then continuing rightwards up steeper ground and then onto the terrace itself. (see map on page 118).

Descent - The easiest descent from the summit of the mountain is via the South Ridge. It is also possible to scramble down North Gully then Little Gully (as shown).

The fantastic scramble of **North Buttress, Mod** *weaves its way up the left side of the crag and can offer an easier alternative if time is of the essence.*

❶ Belle Vue Bastion . . . . ☆2 ☐ **VS 4c**

Great rock, exhilarating moves and breath-taking exposure.
1) 4c, 25m. Gain the right-hand end of the large terrace halfway up North Gully. This is best accessed via Little Gully. Belay just right of a large block. Climb up right and go round the arete. Climb a slab to a small ledge then follow the steep slab above. Continue up the curving groove to a large ledge.
2) 4b, 40m. Head right, air beneath your feet, onto the nose. Climb straight up to easier ground leading to the top. Superb.
FA. I.Waller, C.Palmer 1927

❷ Grooved Arete . . . . ☆3 ☐ **VDiff**

One of the best and most popular routes of its grade in the UK. Start beneath the well-worn corner with the letters 'GA' scratched on the rock.
1) 30m. Climb the corner for 12m, make a move rightwards and then trend left up the slab above to gain a rib leading to a large spike belay.
2) 30m. Step left and follow the prominent rib to a good stance below a corner with a capping roof.
3) 50m. Climb the corner on the right-hand side, passing the awkward capping roof on the right side. Continue more easily leftwards and scramble up to a path.
4) 15m. Walk rightwards along the path to belay at the well-used rocky rib.
5) 38m. Start on the right of the rib and climb up and leftwards to gain the groove above. Follow this until a step left gains a steeper continuation-groove. Climb this until a move leftwards gains a good ledge, block belay well back.
6) 18m. The infamous 'Knight's Move' pitch. How's your chess? Climb the crack behind the belay to reach the slab above. Exit this slab in the top right corner, step round the arete to find a comfortable stance.
7) 20m. Romp up the corner above the belay to reach a good stance.
8) 30m. Head right and climb the steep rock to an ever easing finish. An escape rightwards is easy if the weather is bad or darkness is closing in.
FA. E.Steeple, G.Barlow, A.Doughty, H.Bowron, A.Woodhead 1911

Little Gully

Scramble
descent

North Gully

North Buttress (Mod)

1

2

Tremadog

Cwm Silyn

Cloggy

Llanberis

Lliwedd

Ogwen

Carneddau

Bethesda y Coed

Welsh Winter

① Boot Crack .... 🎟 ☐ HVS 5a
A great boot-sized crack.
22m. Follow the crack. Abseil descent.
FA. A.Moulam, G.Roberts 1966

② Crazy Horse .... 🎟 ☐ E3 6a
A good route with a technical second pitch.
1) 5c, 20m. Climb the worrying large flake
to gain the ledge, belay in the corner.
2) 6a, 30m. Move right, follow the thin
crack to gain an arete and then a tree belay.
3) 5a, 12m. Climb the crack behind the tree.
FA. J.Harwood, A.Sharp 1983

③ Soapgut ...... 🎟 ☐ HS 4b
The slippery corner offers a fine line. The
second pitch shown is **Chimney Route**,
which offers a more fitting finale.
1) 4b, 30m. Climb the corner, often damp,
until a stride round the arete finds a belay.
2) 4a, 15m. Move right to the crack and
follow this and easier climbing to the top.
FA. J.M.Edwards, C.Noyce 1936

④ Wrinkled Retainer
.... 🎟 🧗 🎟 ☐ E5 6c
A tough and green route. Used to be E4
before someone chopped down the starting
tree - not a practice to be encouraged!
30m. A boulder problem start gains the difficult groove which is followed to the top.
FA. J.Redhead, C.Shorter 1980

⑤ Crosscut ... 🎟 🧗 ☐ E2 5b
A wandering line taking-in some of the best
rock on the buttress.
1) 5b, 30m. Climb the easy right corner
until a traverse left gains the niche on the
Wrinkled Retainer. Continue leftwards round
the arete to gain a thin crack and then an
optional belay up and left, part way up the
final pitch of *Soapgut*.
2) 4a, 8m. Finish as for pitch 2 of *Soapgut*.
FA. J.Yates, M.Boysen 1979

Tremadog

Cwm Silyn

Craggy

Llanberis

Lliwedd

Ogwen

Carneddau

Bets y Coed

Welsh Winter

3

4   5

Soapgut

The left side of Milestone Buttress offers some morning sun and a few more-difficult routes if you've polished off the VDiffs on the right.

Approach - Park in the layby beneath the crag, opposite the lake. A short walk up next to the wall leads to the base of the cliff.

Descent - Some of the routes are best descended by abseil. For those that require a walk-off, head right across the top of the crag to descend the steep and often wet gully to the right of *Pulpit Route*.

① Super Direct. . . . . ❀3 ☐ HVS 5a

Fantastic slab-moves on some of the best mountain rock in Wales.

1) 4c, 32m. Climb the polished wall to reach the overlap. Pass this to gain the perfect crack in the rounded rib. Follow this to the ledge.

2) 4c, 30m. Climb a short wall to gain the airy arete. Climb this to gain the large bay.

3) 5a, 22m. A difficult and committing pitch. Traverse left across flaky crimps to gain the niche and follow a crack to the top.

FA. G.Barlow, H.Priestley-Smith 1910. FA. (Final pitch) J.M.Edwards 1941

② Direct Route. . . . . ❀3 ☐ VDiff

A classic outing, described here with a more-direct start up the crack. The original start climbs the diagonal corner on the left.

1) 32m. Start at the polished finger-crack in the centre of the slab. Follow this to gain the diagonal overlap which is followed rightwards to a niche. Gain the slab on the left and make a tricky manoeuvre onto the large ledge.

2) 30m. Climb the large cracked groove behind the belay to reach a large flake. Move left and continue up the groove, moving left again to reach the large bay. If in doubt follow the polish!

3) 12m. The crux chimney! Squirm up the chimney at the back of the bay. Some holds on the right wall might be useful. An alternative, easier finish climbs the wall on the right.

FA. G.Barlow, H.Priestley-Smith 1910

③ Rowan Route . . . . ❀1 ☐ Diff

Another fantastic and amenable classic with solid belays and expansive ledges.

1) 25m. Follow the rib just right of the gully to gain a large ledge with blocks and spikes.

2) 18m. Move right and follow an open groove to a ledge. Take the rib above to gain another good ledge and belay.

3) 15m. Climb slabby rock to gain a chimney above. Follow a chimney to a slab belay.

4) 25m. Scramble straight up to easier ground.

FA. H.Jones, K.Orton, Mrs Orton 1910

④ Pulpit Route. . . . . ❀2 ☐ VDiff

Just left of the descent gully lies this interesting and varied route. Another good one for those with limited multipitch-experience or those who enjoy comfortable belay ledges.

1) 28m. Climb the rib on large holds to reach a good ledge beneath the towering block.

2) 28m. Move left on the large ledge and climb the slab to a runnel. Follow this to a ledge.

3) 12m. Scramble rightwards along the ledge to beneath the gaping chimney.

4) 15m. Climb the chimney, steep at first, to an exit through a hole on the right.

5) 10m. Climb easily up the rib above to the top.

FA. G.Barlow, E.Barlow 1911

Tremadog

Cwm Silyn

Cloggy

Llanberis

Lliwedd

Ogwen

Carnedddau

Betws y Coed

Welsh Winter

Descent Gully

Tremadog

Cwm Silyn

Cloggy

Llanberis

Lliwedd

Ogwen

Carneddau

Betws y Coed

Welsh Winter

Direct Route

The right-hand side of Milestone Buttress gets a lot of afternoon sunshine and also a lot of climbing traffic.
Descent - The steep and often wet gully just right of *Pulpit Route* is the most common descent. Care is needed in the upper reaches, as a slip could prove very serious.

2

3

4

Descent

Late afternoon | 20 min

Tremadog | Cwm Silyn | Clogwy | Llanberis | Lliwedd | **Ogwen** | Carneddau | Berwyn Gerrig | Welsh Winter

2

4 | 4 | 5 | 7

3 | 6

1

Bochlwyd Buttress

A lovely little crag that gets evening sun and dries quickly.
Approach - The crag is approached by taking a small track over the stream from the steep section of the path leading into Glyder Fach main crag. See map on page 118.
Descent - The best descent from the crag is to follow the easy path down the right side of the crag.

1 Wall Climb . . . . ☆ ☐ HS 4b

A great introduction to the harder routes on the main wall, but tough for the grade.

1) 4b, 22m. Climb the initial easy slab to gain the left leading ramp. Make an airy step left and then climb steeper rock to a good niche-belay.

2) 4b, 22m. Climb steeply up and right (often damp), being mindful of some suspect holds, to gain the upper slab and a delightful finish.

FA. F.Hicks, C.Cooper, W.Woosnam Jones 1929

2 Bochlwyd Eliminate

. . . . ☆ 🧗 🔖 ☐ HVS 5a

A fantastically technical wall-climb on great rock. A long, sustained pitch.

40m. Start as for *Wall Climb*, heading straight up where that route strides left. Move up and right to gain a standing position on the narrow ledge. Weave up the wall fairly directly (many options exist) keeping an eye out for the sometimes hard-to-find protection.

FA. R.James, R.Barbier 1962

3 The Wrack

. . . . . . ☆ 🧗 📷 🔖 ☐ E2 5b

A tough, but superbly satisfying route.

40m. An easy start leads to the steep and bold groove. Climb this to gain a ledge. Follow the groove above to finish on the upper slab. Super climbing and great rock.

FA. T.F.Allen, W.Hunford 1963

4 Chimney Climb . . ☆ ☐ S

A steep and traditional outing.

1) 15m. Climb the steep chimney and the face of the block on the left to gain the ledge (awkward). An alternative start on the left is possible.

2) 25m. Squirm up the chimney to the top.

FA. F.Aldous, A.Adams, O.Thorneycroft 1909

5 Two Pitch Route . ☆ ☐ S

The central line gives a worthwhile outing.

1) 28m. Climb directly up the wall right of the chimney. A small step left gains a shallow corner that is followed to a ledge and belay.

2) 22m. Move left over broken ground to climb the left wall via the easiest route.

FA. C.Kirkus, R.Frost 1935

6 Five Pitch Route ☆ ☐ S

Best climbed in one or two pitches!

1) 7m. The easy lower slab.

2) 9m. Step up into the niche and exit left to belay by a good crack.

3) 9m. Climb up and right to a good ledge.

4) 10m. Zig leftwards along the ledge to a weakening, then zag back right to a ledge.

5) 10m. Climb straight up through the bulge to gain the easy upper slab.

FA. C.Kirkus, R.Frost 1935

7 Marble Slab . . . ☆ ☐ HS 4b

A great route with a hard, well protected crux.

40m. Climb the cracked wall to the right of the slab of rock at the base of the crag to the overlap. Pull through this to gain a single crack in the upper headwall. Make tough moves past this to easier climbing above and a ledge. 'Beached-whale' off the ledge via a weakness to an easier finish up the final slab.

FA. C.Kirkus, C.Brennand 1935

8 Arete and Slab . . ☆ ☐ Diff

The easiest route on the crag, and also one of the best. Great positions and varied climbing.

1) 18m. Climb the steep cracked arete on juggy holds to a ledge.

2) 8m. Step left and follow good holds onto the next ledge.

3) 12m. Follow the upper wall of *Marble Slab*.

FA. C.Palmer, D.MacDonald 1927

Tremadog
Cwm Silyn
Cloggy
Llanberis
Lliwedd
Ogwen
Carneddau
Betws y Coed
Welsh Winter

Direct Route

Dolmen Butress

Hawk's Nest

Alphabet Slab   Main Gully   West Gully

❶ Alpha . . . . 🏔️☐ VS 4b
30m. The left edge of the slab is bold.
FA. S.Hereford, J.Laycock 8.1913

❷ Gamma . . . . ☆ 🏔️☐ S 4a
1) 30m. Trend left up the slab following the line of weakness past a scoop and up a crack to a stance. Pro is a bit sparse.
2) 12m. Finish up the tricky wall above.
FA. C.Kirkus, G.Macphee 1936

Glyder Fach
A fine set of mountain cliffs that are in their best condition in warm weather.
Approach - From Ogwen Cottage, take the main path, keeping left towards Tryfan. Pass Llyn Bochlwyd on its left, then break out rightwards to below the buttress.

Late afternoon   60 min

Delta (Diff)

Beta (Mod)

1

2

Tremadog | Cwm Silyn | Cloggy | Llanberis | Lliwedd | Ogwen | Carneddau | Betws y Coed | Welsh Winter

Dolmen Buttress
A well-grooved tower perched high on the right-hand side of this section of the cliff
Approach - Traverse right from above Hawk's Nest or scramble up West Gully then break out left.
Descent - Drop rightwards off the back of the buttress into West Gully and scramble down this.

Hidden chimney

③ Route II . . . . Diff
1) 30m. Worthwhile, on good rock. Up the left of the crest for 8m then move right and climbs past a small ledge (possible stance) before trending back left to reach the terrace.
2) 20m. The deep chimney is a contrast. Rucksacks and helmets may be a hindrance.
FA. E.Steeple, G.Barlow, A.Doughty 9.1914

④ Druid Route . . . . S 4b
1) 18m. The slanting groove leads to a steep corner and an exit left.

2) 16m. The crack and corner at the back of the ledge are the way on.
3) 16m. The slabby angle leads to easy ground and the top of the buttress.
FA. G.Norman, I.Bennett 1949

⑤ Route I . . . . Diff
1) 20m. Up the crack and groove until it is possible to exit rightwards. Move round right to a belay at the foot of a chimney.
2) 10m. Up the chimney to a good ledge.
3) 22m. A cracked groove then the slabby rib on the right concludes things
FA. G.Barlow, R.Henderson, Mrs E.Daniells 1912

Tremadog · Cwm Silyn · Cloggy · Llanberis · Llïwedd · Ogwen · Carneddau · Betws y Coed · Welsh Winter

Ogwen

Main Gully
descent route -
care needed

Tremadog
Cwm Silyn
Cloggy
Llanberis
Lliwedd
Ogwen
Carneddau
Betws y Coed
Welsh Winter

Late afternoon
60 min

1
2
3
4
5

134

❶ Slab Climb . . . . . ⏍ ☐ **VDiff**

A neat excursion spiralling up the left-hand side of the face. The route has long been popular with beginners. It is described with the *Spiral Variant* which avoids the tricky slab on the direct version of Pitch 2 and 3.

1) 15m. Up the rib then move across left to a stance below a chimney with twin 'horns'.
2) 10m. Gain the chimney on the left awkwardly then up and exit leftwards to a stance.
3) 10m. Climb to a ledge then up the tricky crack on the right to a belay.
4) 12m. Move right 3m to a slab and up to the jammed flake of the Arch and a junction with the *The Direct Route* just before its famous hand traverse.
5) 14m. Up the groove on the left on huge flakes to a leftwards exit to an airy stance.
6) 12m. Finish up the rib to reach the top.
FA. K.Ward, H.Gibson 1907

❷ Direct Route . . . ⏍ ☐ **HS 4b**

A classic outing, varied and interesting with a devious but logical line. Popular and with only a couple of hard section - the hand traverse on P4 and the final pitch.

1) 4a, 28m. Climb up the rib and cross over right beneath some blocks. Climb up through these to a grassy ledge with a huge bollard.
2) 4a, 20m. Climb the corner, then move delicately leftwards out across the face beneath before striding round the arete to the jammed flake of the Arch. Belay further left.
2a) Gibson's Chimney, VS 4c, 16m. Good but bold towards the top
3) 4b, 20m. Gain a ledge on the right then move up and swing across the hand traverse to ledges above Gibson's Chimney. Continue to a grand stance on the ledge of Veranda.
4) 4c, 20m. Move right along the ledge to the finish; the wide awkward Coffin Chimney and superb groove of the Final Crack, a good effort for 1907.
4a) VDiff, 18m. The Winter Finish. Move left along the flakes and up the corner to the top.
FA. K.Ward, H.Gibson 1907

Direct Route

A fine bastion of Chamonix-style granite, with a great selection of fine lower and mid grade routes.
Approach - Do a route on Alphabet Slab or walk up the gully just to the left.
Descent - Scramble rightwards over the top of the buttress then descend the wide Main Gully back to the base of the face.

❸ Lot's Wife . . . . . ⏍ ☐ **VS 4c**

A good route taking a great line up the cracked right-hand face of the grand pillar.
1) 30m. Climb the rib and crack to belay just below the overhangs.
2) 4c, 30m. Climb over the small roof and up the groove (crux) then move left onto the rib and left again to access the crack. Follow this past a small ledge, move right and take the slanting groove to the Verandah.
3) 4c, 15m. Finish up Direct Route, or select one of the variations further left.
FA. C.Kirkus, A.Robinson 1931

❹ Lot's Groove . . . ⏍ ☐ **HVS**

1) 5a, 30m. A great pitch up the steep shallow groove overlooking the gully. Start from the 1st stance of the Chasm and move out left to reach the groove. Up this, sustained exposed and excellent with good protection throughout. Finish up *Lot's Wife*.
FA. C.Kirkus, A.Robinson 1929

❺ Chasm Route . . . ⏍ ☐ **VDiff**

The character building rifts on the right can be climbed in as many as six short pitches.
1) 26m. Climb the rib and crack then move right into the base of the mighty rift.
2) 20m. Up the chasm until an exit right is possible. Head left over blocks back to the gully.
3) 20m. A crack on the left leads to flakes. Go behind these then back right into the gully.
4) 20m. Do battle with the jaws of the Vertical Vice then finish up the corner above.
FA. J.Thompson, H.Jones, L.Noon 1910

❶ Get Close .... ⬜ HVS 5a
1) 20m. Climb the left-hand side-wall via crack, until the elegant hanging groove in the rib can be reached. Climb this to finish.
FA. L.Hardy, C.Parkin 1989

❷ The Hollow Men ...... ⬜ E1 5b
The steep groove round to the right of the impressive hanging rib is also worth seeking out.
1) 20m. Climb the groove to a ledge then continue up the final section by strenuous manoeuvres.
FA. A.Newton, M.Crook 1985

❸ Hawks Nest Arete......... ⬜ VS 4c
Fine climbing based around the dramatic square cut arete.
1) 4c, 30m. Steady climbing leads to a large flake perched on the arete then harder and bolder moves reach the sanctuary of a small ledge. Shuffle right to a shallow chimney-slot and up this to a flake that leads out left onto the wall. A good ledge is just above.
2) 14m. The slabby crack leads to the top.
FA. P.Nock, H.Harrisnon 1940

❹ Hawks Nest Buttress.... ⬜ S 4b
The original route of the buttress trends left to right to find the easiest line. Steady climbing though the crucial mantelshelf is a bit of a stopper.
1) 16m. Trend right up slabby rock to a spike belay
2) 4b, 16m. Move round right then climb the slot to a jammed block before making a hard mantelshelf out right. Belay in the recess just a little higher.
3) 26m. Climb easy rock then the chimney behind the tower of blocks and flakes to reach open ground and the top.
FA. G.Abraham, A.Abraham, A.Thompson 1905

Late afternoon

60 min

Tremadog

Cwm Silyn

Cloggy

Llanberis

Lliwedd

Ogwen

Carneddau

Betws y Coed

Welsh Winter

Descent past the base of Dolmen Buttress

Hawk's Nest Buttress

A chunky and striking arete perched above steep ground, offering good climbing in a grand setting.
Approach - Traverse right from above Alphabet Stab or scramble up broken ground to the face.
Descent - Trend right across ledge to the foot of Dolmen Buttress then descend West Gully.

3   4

① Scimitar Crack .... 🏁 🖌️ ☐ VS 4c

A short but perfectly formed route tucked away on the left side of the buttress.

1) 4c, 25m. Follow the small rightward-facing groove until it runs out. Karate-chop your way up the excellent jamming crack above.

2) 20m. Scramble up and right to join *Sub Cneifion Rib* on its second pitch or escape by scrambling left.

FA. M.Creasey 1980

② Sub Cneifion Rib. . . 🏁 🖼️ ☐ VDiff

An immaculate trip following the beautiful barrel of perfect rock. Large belay ledges and easy escape options make this route feel less committing than its Idwal Slab neighbours and it can be a good choice if rain looks imminent. *Photo on page 119.*

1) 30m. A 3 star pitch in its own right. Start below the pointed boulder and follow the groove, crack then slab to the bulge. Pass this on the left (tricky) and finish up the slab to a large belay ledge.

2) 35m. Wander left easily to reach the next true section of climbing. Take the broad rib direct via a crack to reach the rounded-top.

3) 25m. Scramble rightwards to belay below the small roof in the right arete of the rib.

4) 35m. A fitting finale. Rock around the nose to a scoop. Head up and left on the front of the pillar then finish up the crack. An easier finish right can be made.

FA. J.M.Edwards 1931

Tremadog

Cwm Silyn

Clogwyn

Llanberis

Llliwedd

Ogwen

Carneddau

Bettws y Coed

Welsh Winter

Late afternoon | 20 min

Scramble off the back

2

Sub Cneifion Rib

The rounded rib above Llyn Idwal offers a delightful alternative to the main Idwal Slabs adventures. It is possible to scramble off rightwards after the 1st and 2nd pitches if needed.

Approach - As for the approach to Idwal Slabs, but break off the main path near the far end of the Llyn and head uphill on the smaller track direct to the toe of the buttress.

Descent - Drop off the back of the pinnacle and follow the small track down the right side of the buttress.

Idwal Slabs

The Idwal Slabs are deservedly popular. The easy-angled routes have generally good protection and ample belay ledges, however the descent is tricky and may involve an abseil due to its awkward and exposed nature.

Approach (see map on page 118) - Park at Ogwen Cottage and follow the main path up into Cwm Idwal. The Slabs are situated above Llyn Idwal on the left.

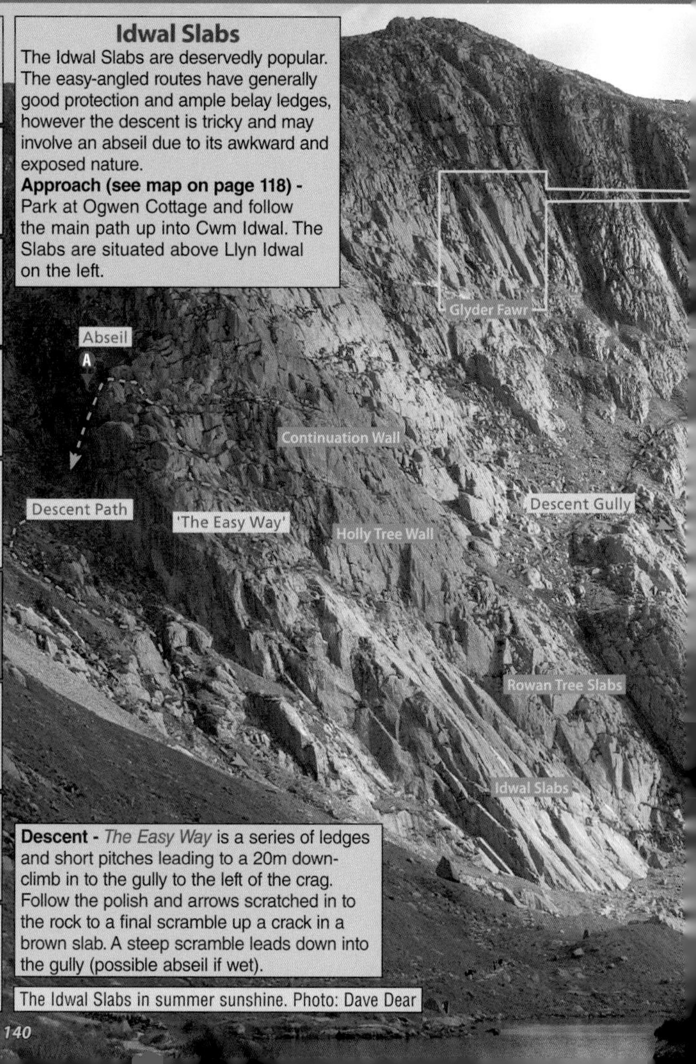

Abseil
A

Glyder Fawr

Continuation Wall

Descent Path

'The Easy Way'

Holly Tree Wall

Descent Gully

Rowan Tree Slabs

Idwal Slabs

Descent - *The Easy Way* is a series of ledges and short pitches leading to a 20m down-climb in to the gully to the left of the crag. Follow the polish and arrows scratched in to the rock to a final scramble up a crack in a brown slab. A steep scramble leads down into the gully (possible abseil if wet).

The Idwal Slabs in summer sunshine. Photo: Dave Dear

Tremadog
Cwm Silyn
Clogwyn
Llanberis
Lliwedd
Ogwen
Carneddau
Betws y Coed
Welsh Winter

Glyder Fawr

A fine sheet of bubbly grey rock set high on the flanks of Glyder Fawr. Either of the two routes described here makes a logical extension to route combos on the slabs and upper walls.
Approach - From above Continuation Wall traverse rightwards to the base of the slabs.
Descent - The least complicated descent is to scramble to the plateau and descend via the Devil's Kitchen path over to the right.

① Grey Slab . . . . VS 4b

Delicate, sustained an excellent. The route is not well protected and is prone to seepage on the initial crack and upper crux - care required if at all damp, especially on the upper part of P2. Once known as *Lost Boot Climb*.
1) 4a, 34m. Start up the corner for 20m then trend left across the bubbly slab to a rib, balance up this to a small stance and high belay under the overlap.
2) 4b, 50m. Climb through the bulge then move left and head up the vague rib to the overlap high above. Jig left and right through this and finish up the final slab, carefully avoiding any wetness.
FA. J.M.Edwards, F.Reade 1932

② Grey Arete . . . . . . HVS 5a

Great rock and superb situations plus delicate climbing up the rib that is the central feature here.
1) 4c, 35m. Climb the groove in the arete and the slab on the right to a good ledge and belays.
2) 5a, 45m. Balance up the bold arete to a ledge (possible stance) then climb the tricky crack that splits the arete and finish up the short wall above.
FA. R.James, P.Benson 1959

Tremadog

Cwm Silyn

Cloggy

Llanberis

Llilwedd

Ogwen

Carneddau

Betws y Coed

Welsh Winter

Continuation Wall

'The Easy Way'

Demetreus
- next page

Faith - next page

1   2   3   4   5   6

Idwal Slabs

Long and classic low grade routes only a short stroll from the road - no wonder the place is popular. Arrive early or be prepared to queue.

Descent - Take the '*Easy Way*' leftwards up a series of well-worn ledges and short risers leading a shoulder. Cross this to locate a 20m down-climb or abseil in to the gully to the left of the crag.

❶ Tennis Shoe . . . ☆☆☆ ☐ HS 4a

A superb route, perched above the steep East Wall. Great positions and rock, though a bit polished in places. Start left of the main slab at a smaller slab tucked in against its edge.

1) 4a, 30m. Climb the subsidiary slab on polished holds to stance on the at its top.

2) 16m. Move right up a scoop onto the main slab and climb its edge to a good ledge.

3) 18m. Continue up the slab to a large flake. Belay here or just left in the open gully

4) 38m. Up the gully then transfer to the rib on the left. Climb this on its left edge to a ledge.

5) 40m. Easier climbing leads to a grass terrace. Walk left to below the final rock tower.

6) 4a, 15m. Climb up past a scoop (delicate and slippery) to gain the slab above. Pull for glory over the perched block to finish!

FA. N.Odell (in his pumps) 1919

❷ Direct Route ☆☆ 🖾 ☐ HVS 4c

45m. A great alternative if you are up to it, though as the grade suggests, it is delicate and bold with virtually no gear. Climb the scoop until it steepens then balance out right to gain and climb the slab.

❸ Ordinary Route ☆ 🖐 ☐ Diff

The easiest route here gives a memorable trip up the 'trench' and 'goes' in all weathers.

1) 45m. Follow the well-worn boot-crack to a niche and a belay.

2) 46m. Move over left to gain and follow the rightward-trending scoop.

3) 25m. Follow the polished crack to the large ledge and various belays

4) 25m. Head left for 8m then back right to the terrace below the upper walls.

FA. T.Rose, C.Moss 1897

❹ Charity . . . . ☆☆ ☐ VDiff

Another long-time classic with the sheen to prove how well loved it has been.

1) 38m. Climb the slippery scoop and at its top exit right. Quartz spangled rock leads left then right to a terrace.

2) 26m. Climb the groove and slab to more quartzy rock. Up this leftwards to a stance.

3) 16m. Climb rightwards up the white highway to a stance in a corner.

4) 30m. Skip up the corner, which can be quite tricky in the wet.

5) 28m. Wander up to belay on the ledges above the slabs.

FA. D.Pye, I.Richards, T.Picton 1916

❺ Central Rib . . . . ☆ ☐ S 4a

45m. A neat variation start to the routes to either side.

❻ Hope . . . . ☆☆ ☐ VDiff

Probably the most classic of the classics here and one of the most popular routes in Wales. The polished nature of the holds makes it a good bit harder in the wet.

1) 45m. A quartzy slab leads to ledges and an A-shaped niche in the overlap. Pull through this, more slab work then leads to a stance.

2) 25m. The glossy twin-cracks give skiddy work (good runners) to a flake, step left and continue to a stance in a corner.

3) 20m. More neat climbing on nice crinkly holds leads to a stance in the groove.

4) 28m. Climb the groove and sidestep the bulge leftwards, to reach ledgy ground.

5) 18m. Continue until things rear up and an escape left is required.

FA. E.Daniells, I.Richards, T.Roxburgh, R.Henderson 1915

❻ **Faith** . . . . 🏳 ⬜ **VDiff**

The right-hand of the trio of saintly routes is often damp, though it is still well worthwhile. Start under the right-hand sheet of slab where its undercut base ends.

1) 35m. Step then trend left up the edge of the slab before heading direct to a big stance.

2) 30m. Follow the quartz rails out left to a crack and head up this to belay.

3) 16m. An easy groove leads to a stance under the West Wall.

4) 28m. Climb leftwards onto the next sheet of slab then tiptoe up its left edge to a stance. A neat pitch.

5) 25m. More broken ground leads up then left to reach the large terrace below the upper walls. Escape left along the 'Easy Way' or continue on upwards.

FA. D.Pye, I.Richards, T.Picton 1916

❼ **Demetreus** . . 🏳 ⬜ **E3 6a**

Reached by climbing Faith (or Hope) this fine pitch gives fantastic and gripping climbing up a clean tower of perfect rock.

25m. The vague crack/seam provides pretty much the only option up the wall. Climb it until it disappears, then stop thinking and sprint for the top.

FA. D.Beetlestone, G.Gibson 1979

❽ **Rowan Tree Slabs**

. . . . 🏳 ⬜ **E2 5c**

Absorbing climbing up the steep side wall that rises above the main slabs. It is reached by the first pitch of *Faith*.

1) 5c, 32m. Wander up to the steeper face and access a tiny quartz ledge. Teeter along this leftwards then climb the slab leftwards, bold and hard, past a 'porthole' with more hard moves to the sanctuary of a ledge.

2) 5b, 14m. Move left to a groove in the arete to a small ledge and finish up the wall.

FA. J.O'Neill 1963. Most of the main pitch had been climbed by F.Hicks in 1929.

Continuation Wall

Easy Way

Rowan Tree Slabs

The West Wall of the Idwal Slabs is home to a couple of superb and tough challenges. The thin crack of *Demetreus* is not to be missed, and the open delicacy of *Rowan Tree Slabs* is also excellent! The much milder offering of *Faith* is also described here.

Approach - The two hard routes are approached up the lower slabs.

Descent - Traverse right beyond the sidewall to reach open ground. Either descend a gully down the buttress on the right or traverse horizontally until clear of the crags and descend the scree. (See overview on page 140).

Tremadog | Cwm Silyn | Cloggy | Llanberis | Lliwedd | Ogwen | Carneddau | Betws-y-Coed | Welsh Winter

Not much sun

20 min

Tremadog

Cwm Silyn

Cloggy

Llanberis

Lliwedd

Ogwen

Carneddau

Betws-y-Coed

Welsh Winter

Descent

7

8

6

Hope - previous page

Descent

Descent

7

8

9 10 11

1

2

3

'The Easy Way'

4

5

6

Idwal Slabs

Late afternoon

20 min

Holly Tree Wall and Continuation Wall

Above the laid back routes of the Idwal Slabs lie two steeper tiers of quality rock. The rapid drying nature and wonderful setting make up for their lack of stature. Routes here make a logical extension to any of those below.

Approach - Any of the lower routes lead to the terrace below Holly Tree Wall.

Descent - Scramble left to reach the upper section of *The Easy Way*.

❶ Rampart Corner

E1 5c

A good pitch up the shallow groove cleaving the cleanest piece of rock here.

35m. Climb the groove then traverse left and pull through the roof to access the soaring shallow corner. This gives interesting sustained climbing with good gear throughout.
FA. H.Banner, R.Wilson 1977

❷ Original Route VS 5a

A top-notch lead for 1918 and a great route.

1) 5a, 28m. Boulder into the groove in the centre of the face then follow the slab rightwards to access a narrow chimney-crack. Up this to a ledge.

2) 4b, 10m. Plod up the crack above.
FA. I.Richards, C.Holland, D.Pilley 1918

❸ Piton Route . . . . VS 4b

A fine open climb with good positions. An escape in to *Lazarus* is possible.

35m. Climb into the short groove and exit right to polished ledges (possible stance). Continue up the crack past another ledge to a finish through a short bulge.
FA. F.Hicks, W.Woosnam-Jones 1929

❹ Lazarus . . . . . . HS 4a

The easiest line hereabouts and a logical continuation to *Tennis Shoe*. Start from the grassy ledges in the base of *Javelin* gully.

1) 4a, 12m. Three mini-mantels up the gully lead to a stance where it widens.

2) 4a, 28m. Traverse left towards a jutting nose of rock and climb the groove to its right.

❺ Javelin Buttress . VS 4c

34m. Climb the groove that splits the buttress and a scoop to a thread. Layback and mantel onto the upper slab and wander up this, easing all the time.
FA. F.Graham, C.Jerram 1925

❻ Javelin Blade E1 5b

One of the UK's very 1st 'Extreme' routes.

34m. Follow the *Buttress* to the thread then move left towards the arete and climb the shallow groove of 'the blade' - bold and precarious - to easier ground. Excellent.
FA. J.Longland, C.Williams 1930

The highest and final wall above the Idwal Slabs is a lofty home to many great routes.

❼ The Arete . . . . . . VDiff

25m. Start up the groove then trend left to the well-positioned edge of the slab.
FA. F.Hicks, C.Warren, A.Spence 1929

❽ The Upper Staircase Diff

18m. The awkward big-booted groove.

❾ Continuation Crack HVS 5a

18m. The crack in the face past threads - neat.

❿ Groove Above S 4a

10m. Gain the groove with difficulty, up it to bulges then escape right.
FA. T.Knowles, H.Poole 1926

⓫ Diagonal Route . HVS 5a

18m. Climb twin crack then cross *Groove Above* to finish up the rounded arete.

Tremadog · Cwm Silyn · Clogwy · Llanberis · Lliwedd · Ogwen · Carneddau · Betws y Coed · Welsh Winter

There are two excellent isolated buttresses near Ogwen where you are almost guaranteed solitude. Carnedd y Filiast has two beautifully situated slabs with a set of fine easier routes on clean rock. A steep approach-walk adds to the day.

Braich Ty Du is closer to the road and has a great ridge route.

Bethesda

Snowdon Mountain Lodge

P

A5

Tal-newyddion (Don't park at the house)

Braich Ty Du

Carnedd y Filiast

GPS 53.123418 -4.020018

P

Ogwen Cottage

Sam James following *Left Edge* (VDiff) - *page 151* - on Carnedd y Filiast. Photo: Alan James

Tremadog / Cwm Silyn / Cloggy / Llanberis / Lliwedd / Ogwen / Carneddau / Betws y Coed / Welsh Winter

① Pinnacle Ridge Route . . . . VDiff

A fun outing that lies close to the A5 and catches sun for much of the day. The first pitch sports lovely rock and the final traverse negotiates some interesting gendarmes not unlike an alpine ridge. Start at the base of the ridge close to the letters PR scratched in the rock.

1) 40m. Follow the right hand of the two ribs on wonderful clean rock to a steep blocky section that leads to a heathery terrace.

2) 15m. Follow easier ground to gain a good spike belay on a ledge.

3) 22m. Traverse right and climb the ridge to another ledge.

4) 20m. Follow the crested ridge to gain easy ground.

FA. K.U.Ingold, P.J.Fearon, J.M.Ball 1950

Lots of sun / 20 min

Descent gully off to the right

Braich Ty Du

Approach - From the parking at Ogwen Cottage on the A5, cross the road and gain the hillside under the crag via the stile. A faint path can be followed leftwards and it is possible to contour round to beneath the route.
Descent - Continue up the hill to a grassy col and then follow a broad easy gully on the right of the crag.

Carnedd y Filiast

A remote set of slabs which has some great easy routes. Peace and quiet is almost guaranteed.

Approach (see map on page 148) - Park near the house at Tal-newyddion (don't park at the house). Walk north (away from Ogwen) down the road past the house and gain the field (boggy) on the left. Skirt back around behind the house to the wall and follow a steep path up the hillside into the cwm. There is no access to this path from directly behind the house.

Descent - Walk down the hillside rightwards (looking in) and scramble back down to the wall by the approach path.

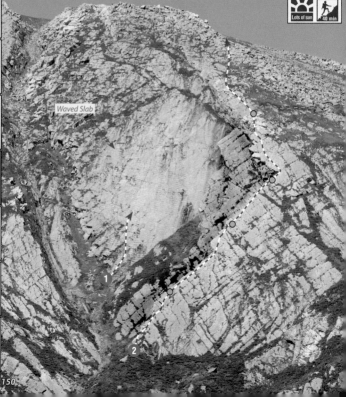

Waved Slab

Tremadog

Cwm Silyn

Cloggy

Llanberis

Lliwedd

Ogwen

Carneddau

Betws y Coed

Welsh Winter

① Waved Slab . . . . □ Mod
This beautiful slab can be climbed virtually anywhere at an easy standard but there are few runners or belay ledges. Doing it in one long 60m pitch can help.

② Left Edge . . . . 🏃2 □ VDiff
A fine route in a magnificent position. The stances are small and the gear is not always where you want it but the slab is easy-angled and the climbing is generally very straightforward.
1) 30m. Start at the left toe of the protruding buttress to the right of the clean *Waved Slab*. Follow the edge fairly directly to a *small* stance. *Photo on page 148.*
2) 45m. The same line leads to an even *smaller* stance by three large blocks.
3) 30m. Continue to the *smallest* stance just before the slab angles back left.
4) 45m. More good slab climbing leads to a bigger ledge at the top. Exit right at this point or continue via another pitch upwards to reach easy ground and the ridge above.

③ Central Route . . . . 🏃2 □ S
This delightful route takes the best line of clean rock. The climbing is relatively easy for the grade but it is thin on gear in places.
1) 35m. Climb direct up the seam 2m left of the right-facing corner of the *Underlap*.
2) 40m. Continue in the same line as the angle gradually eases towards the top.
FA. F.Graham 1924

④ Underlap . . . . 🏃1 □ VDiff
The right-facing scoop just right of the centre of the slab gives good climbing.
1) 40m. Follow the scoop then move up and left to belay at the base of a corner.
2) 35m. Climb the corner - dirty in places - to the top.

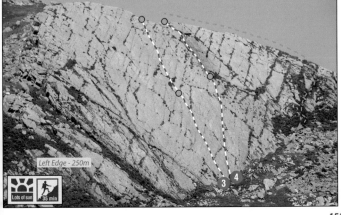

Left Edge - 250m

Lots of sun | 35 min

Tremadog | Cwm Silyn | Cloggy | Llanberis | Lliwedd | Ogwen | Carneddau | Betws y Coed | Welsh Winter

Carneddau

Tremadog

Cwm Silyn

Cloggy

Llanberis

Lliwedd

Ogwen

Carneddau

Betws y Coed

Welsh Winter

Tremadog

Cwm Silyn

Cloggy

Llanberis

Lliwedd

Ogwen

Carneddau

Betws y Coed

Welsh Winter

Wild Horses in the Carneddau. Photo: Mick Ryan

The brooding mountains of the Carneddau flank the Ogwen valley on the east side. The rolling nature of the hills cry out 'wilderness' and the crags are amongst the quietest in North Wales. We have included some less-frequented crags such as Carreg Mianog, which offers relatively easy access sunny rock and is a great alternative venue for avoiding the crowds.

Approach

The approaches for the crags of the Carneddau all begin from the main A5 road through the Ogwen valley. Some of the crags such as Craig yr Ysfa have the longest walk-ins in the area, but with that come some of the best views. For Craig Lloer, park either in the laybys by the start of the path up, or at Gwen Gof Uchaf. For the other crags park at the Gwern Gof Isaf campsite. A small fee is payable if parking at either of the farmhouses.

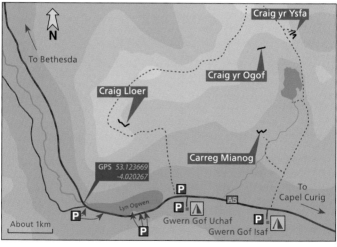

Conditions

Carreg Mianog is a low lying, quick drying crag which receives a lot of sun. It is very gritstonesque in stature. The rest of the crags are summer venues as they can be quite damp and cold unless the weather is good. It is not uncommon to be wearing hats and gloves up at Craig yr Ysfa in midsummer!

Jack Geldard on *Biceps Wall* (VS) - *page 159* - Carreg Mianog. Photo: Sophie Evitt

① Kirkus's Route .... VS 5a

The fine central offwidth provides a mighty struggle on an unsung Welsh gem.
1) 4a, 25m. 5m left of the lowest point of the buttress is a chimney. Follow this past a small ledge to gain a slabby groove on the right. Climb this and move left to belay on a grassy ledge.
2) 5a, 20m. Gain the offwidth-crack which looms above and fight up it using the chockstones for protection and holds, a big cam might be useful but is a little unsporting. Belay at the top of the crack.
3) 4a, 25m. Move right to the rib and climb this until a stride left gains a square cut groove. Follow this to a belay on easier ground.
4) 15m. Scramble off.
FA. C.Kirkus 1928

Descent

Eastern Arete Diff

② The Rib .... S

A nice route, making the most of the pleasant rock on the rib, and avoiding the vegetation in the grooves. Start at a detached block leaning against the main crag.
1) 26m. Up over the block and follow a chimney to gain a tricky move left to a ledge. Scramble back and left to belay in the corner.
2) 20m. Move right to gain the rib proper and follow it until a belay in the right-hand groove can be reached.
3) 30m. Gain the arete on the left which is followed to a groove and then the top.
FA. L.Holliwell, J.Rodgers 1971

Craig Lloer

A quiet, peaceful and picturesque cwm.

Descent - The gully behind and left of the crag (behind *Eastern Arete*) provides a straight-forward descent.

③ Central Ridge . . ☆ ☐ **HS 4a**

A good route, and when combined with an ascent of *Kirkus's Route* gives a varied and often solitary mountain day-out. The route is loosely based on the broken central rib of rock.

1) 28m. Climb blocky ground to gain a crack. Follow this and move left to gain the rib. Climb the rib, various belays possible.

2) 20m. Follow the broken rib until a ledge is reached below the final steep wall.

3) 4a, 32m. Climb the rib to gain a leftward traverse on a narrow ledge. From here climb the difficult groove above and exit leftwards.

FA. I.Clayton, B.Cooke 1953

④ North Arete . . . . ☆ ☐ **Diff**

A great romp with large holds, nice positions and ample belays. Start just left of the overhanging buttress at a short chimney.

1) 22m. Climb the initial chimney, then easier ground to belay at the quartzy patch.

2) 35m. Romp up the main rib above on beautiful rock to gain a ledge beneath the final steepening.

3) 20m. Follow the crack above the belay and regain the rib proper. Follow this to easier ground.

FA. R.Henderson, E.Danielles 1911

Tremadog

Cwm Silyn

Cloggy

Llanberis

Lliwedd

Ogwen

Carneddau

Betws y Coed

Welsh Winter

Carreg Mianog

Carreg Mianog is a sunny, quick-drying crag that can provide a superb quiet day-out with stunning views of the Ogwen Valley and Tryfan. It has a pioneering feel.

Approach - From the Craig yr Isfa approach, follow the water leat leftwards, passing over a bridge, until beneath the crag. Head up the hillside to the base.

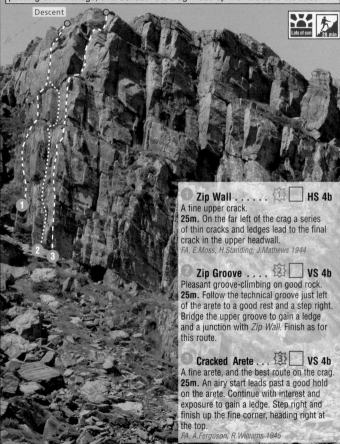

Descent

Lots of sun

20 min

1 Zip Wall . . . . . . ☆1 ☐ HS 4b
A fine upper crack.
25m. On the far left of the crag a series of thin cracks and ledges lead to the final crack in the upper headwall.
FA. E.Moss, H.Standing, J.Mathews 1944

2 Zip Groove . . . . ☆2 ☐ VS 4b
Pleasant groove-climbing on good rock.
25m. Follow the technical groove just left of the arete to a good rest and a step right. Bridge the upper groove to gain a ledge and a junction with *Zip Wall.* Finish as for this route.

3 Cracked Arete . . . ☆3 ☐ VS 4b
A fine arete, and the best route on the crag.
25m. An airy start leads past a good hold on the arete. Continue with interest and exposure to gain a ledge. Step right and finish up the fine corner, heading right at the top.
FA. A.Ferguson, R.Williams 1945

Pectoral Wall ☐ HVS 5a

A worthwhile route.
1) 4c, 16m. An awkward and mossy first wall leads past a crack to a ledge on the left.
2) 5a, 16m. Climb up through the small roof and head left to a crack. Follow this to finish.
FA. J.Whittle, D.Peers 1971

5 Temper .... ☆1 ☐ E2 5c

Atmospheric pulling in the upper roof.
1) 5b, 22m. An eliminate first-wall leads to tough moves to gain the 'cannon'.
2) 5c, 12m. The superb hanging arete above the roof is gained directly via a hard pull.
FA. C.Goodey 1962

Biceps Wall ... ☆2 ☐ VS 4c

A superbly varied route on great rock.
Photo page 155.
1) 4c, 22m. A tough start leads in to a niche at 6m. Follow ledges easily to reach a roof-crack on the right. Burl round this to a ledge on the sticking out 'cannon'.
2) 4c, 12m. Follow the wall above on crimps and a rightward trending line of slopers.
FA. D.Haworth, G.Horridge 1948

Knee Cap .... ☐ VS 4c

A steep groove best climbed in one pitch.
24m. Climb the steep green groove past ledges to reach the final crack.
FA. R.James, R.Roberts 1959

Tremadog

Cwm Silyn

Cloggy

Llanberis

Lliwedd

Ogwen

Carneddau

Betws y Coed

Welsh Winter

Early morning

55 min

Amphitheatre Buttress

A three-star mountaineering classic.
Approach - From the col, descend
rightwards (looking down) and follow a
vague path down the heathery slope.
The path zig-zags downhill, and takes
a gully on the left near the base of the
crag. Contour around the base of the
crag to reach the start of the route.

Approach for *Pinnacle Wall* - page 163

Pinnacle Wall

Mur y

Approach for *Amphitheatre Buttress*

❶ Amphitheatre Buttress . . . . 🕮 ☐ **VDiff**

A long mountain adventure. Never desperate, with stunning views and varied climbing. The route involves some easy scrambling in the midsection, and isn't sustained, but the short tricky sections are 'interesting' and the entire route is over 300m in length. A huge gully drops away beneath Pinnacle Wall. Start 15m above the toe of the buttress that forms the left side of this. The route is not described in individual pitches. *Photo below.*

1) 130m. Pleasant, pocketed slab climbing leads to a ledge at 30m. More slabs lead to a tricky groove, above which more easy slab-climbing leads onto a large ledge beneath a steep wall.

2) 22m. On the right is the crux groove. A polished corner leads to a large detached block. Continue past this to gain easier ground.

3) 75m. Scramble along paths and vegetated ground to reach the crested ridge.

4) 35m. Traverse the apex of the alpine-esque ridge passing two prominent gendarmes.

5) 60m. Follow the ridge on the right to gain the summit.

FA. G.Abraham, A.Abraham, D.Leighton, J.Puttrell 1905

The upper ridge of *Amphitheatre Buttress.*
(VDiff) - *this page*. Photo: Jack Geldard

Pinnacle Wall

The upper wall of Craig y Ysfa is home to some superb and atmospheric mountain-routes.

Approach (see photo on previous page) - From the col, head leftwards up to the summit following the main walkers path. The crag can be accessed via abseil (recommended) or down the main gully via a loose scramble.

A

The Haunted (E5)

3

4

1

2

5

Bilberry Ledge

6

Lower Amphitheatre Wall

Tremadog

Cwm Silyn

Cloggy

Llanberis

Ll\iwedd

Ogwen

Carneddau

Craig yr Ysfa

Welsh Winter

❶ Gettysburg . ☼①◀☐ HVS 5b

A good route with some steep sections and varied climbing. Start on the left of the upper ledge.

1) 5b, 30m. Climb the tricky slab until a step right gains a semi-rest in a niche under the first prominent overhang. Pull through the overhang to gain another, smaller overhang. Strenuous moves round this into a corner lead to yet another overhang which is exited left to a stance.

2) 4c, 22m. Blast up the steep wall behind the belay, trend right and finish over blocky ground.

FA. C.Jones, A.Moulam, R.Conway 1969

❷ The Grimmett ☼②◀☐ VS 4c

A classic steep VS adventure that gives a great outing with acres of exposure.

1) 4c, 30m. Follow the prominent corner to a steepening. Climb steeply leftward to gain another corner which is climbed to a technical move left into a narrow corner. Bridge up this to gain the grassy ledge. Belay on the right.

2) 4b, 20m. Traverse up and left to gain an arete. Swing round this and climb the steep wall to gain a wide crack which leads to the top.

FA. A.Cox, R.Beaumont 1938

❸ Excalibur . . . ☼①🎦☐ E2 5b

A worthwhile route with an energizing swing around the lower arete providing the meat.

1) 5b, 30m. Follow *The Grimmett* until you are above the second overhang. Move right past a small overlap to gain the arete, swing boldly round this to gain a sloping ledge. Climb more easily up to a grassy belay.

2) 5a, 20m. Climb directly behind the stance to gain and climb a groove in the centre of the wall.

FA. M.Crook 1980

❹ Spiral Scratch ☼①🖐☐ E2 5b

A pleasant outing up the inviting pillar of clean rock that hangs just right of *The Grimmett*. Although the technical grade is low for an E2, the route is not one to be underestimated.

1) 5b, 35m. Start as for the previous two routes. At 4m, break right to gain an arete. Climb this and gain the centre of the pillar which is followed, passing a diagonal crack, to the belay.

2) 4c, 18m. Follow the clean arete on the right to reach a good ledge and easy ground.

FA. G.Gibson, A.Hudson, A.Popp 1983

❺ Pinnaclissima . . ☼③☐ E2 5c

A fantastic route, the best on the wall.

1) 5b, 15m. Power up the left facing corner to reach a belay on the right, just above the quartz ledge.

2) 5c, 35m. Stem up the technical corner (small wires) to gain a wide crack. Climb this to a horizontal break 3m below the tip of the pinnacle. Monkey left to finish up *Pinnacle Wall*.

FA. C.Jones, R.Jones 1969

Starting just left of Pinnacle Wall , and finishing direct, is the bold and superb wall climb of **The Haunted (E5 6a)**.

❻ Pinnacle Wall. . . ☼③☐ S 4a

A classic, must-do route that weaves an unlikely line up this fine cliff.

1) 15m. Climb the grassy ramp to a stance.

2) 30m. Climb up 3m to gain the quartzy ledge. Follow this to belay under the groove.

3) 4a, 35m. Climb the groove for 10m then trend right to reach the tip of the pinnacle. Step left and climb the slab above to finish.

FA. C.Kirkus (Solo) 1931

Tremadog

Cwm Silyn

Cloggy

Llanberis

Lliwedd

Ogwen

Carneddau

Bewty-y-Coed

Welsh Winter

① Plumbagin . . . . . ⭐ ▢ **E1 5b**

A fine, if somewhat baffling route.
1) 5b, 18m. Climb the V-chimney to its end. Pull up to a horizontal crack, then scuttle right onto the ledge. Care is required to build a sound belay, small wires useful.
2) 4b, 32m. Move right and gain the groove above with some bamboozling manoeuvres. Follow this to gain Bilberry Ledge.
FA. J.Clements, D.Potts 1965

② Aura . . . . . . ⭐ 🧗 ▢ **E2 5b**

The finest route on the crag, and one of the best E2s in North Wales. Start in a small damp gully.
1) 5b, 45m. Climb straight up to a small triangular overlap at 10m. Climb diagonally left to reach a crack and then trend back right to the base of the long slanting crack. Make a tough move to gain the crack proper and follow it to a belay ledge.
2) 12m. Scramble onto Bilberry Ledge.
FA. R.Carrington, A.Rouse, B.Hall 1975

③ Mur y Niwl . . ⭐ 📷 ▢ **VS 5a**

Another stunning classic with sustained difficulties and breath-taking exposure at the grade. Care is needed to protect the 2nd adequately on the devious and highly exposed crux pitch.
1) 4b, 12m. Climb up to the left side of the large grassy ledge. Walk along the ledge and belay beneath the flakes and corner.
2) 5a, 32m. Climb the wall above the belay to gain the base of the large corner system. Hand traverse rightwards along the highest of two parallel ledges to gain a tough step-down. Follow an easing diagonal line rightwards to an awkward semi-hanging belay stance.
3) 4c, 18m. Drop down rightwards from the stance and head right again under the roof to reach a ledge. Climb up and left, past an arete, to gain a grassy stance.
4) 4c, 22m. Climb the groove above to gain the short cracked wall. Climb the crack.
FA. A.Moulam, J.Churchill 1952

Mur y Niwl

The centre-piece of the crag!
Approach - Either scramble
down the steep, loose gully,
or abseil down Pinnacle Wall,
then down Amphitheatre Wall.

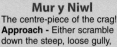

❹ Agrippa   **E1 5a**

A tough and well-named proposition where technique and nerve will stand you in good stead.

1) 5a, 30m. Nip up the leftward slanting groove to gain the ledge. Climb diagonally right to gain another ledge and from the right-hand side of this, climb the wall above to belay on the next ledge.

2) 5a, 18m. Climb straight up the wall above on good holds and step left above the overlap into the groove. Climb this, then traverse right to the ledge.

3) 5a, 25m. Drop down 2m and traverse right to a ledge on the nose of the buttress. Climb rightwards and then head diagonally left past sloping ledges to a grassy ledge.

4) 4c, 40m. Move left on the ledge to climb a steep wall into a groove. This leads to long easy slabs which are followed to the Bilberry Ledge.

FA. J.Wharton, D.Isles (aid) 1959

Tremadog · Cwm Silyn · Cloggy · Llanberis · Lliwedd · Ogwen · **Carneddau** · Betws y Coed · Welsh Winter

165

Craig yr Ogof

An overlooked crag that offers some good low E-grade routes that are worth seeking out.

Descent - The routes finish on easy ground near the top of the crag. Scramble to the very top of the crag and descend the hillside to the left.

Morning | 40 min

Scramble off

1

2

3

4

5

Tremadog | Cwm Silyn | Cloggy | Llanberis | Lliwedd | Ogwen | Carneddau | Betws y Coed | Welsh Winter

❶ Pentangle E2 5c

This strenuous route tackles the pod shaped groove to the right of the oft-damp chimney.
1) 5c, 30m. Tackle the steep break to gain access to the pod on the right. Climb the pod to an overhang, then make a swing right to gain a good crack that leads to the top of the large flake.
2) 4a, 20m. Step right and climb a short steep wall and a mossy slab to gain the large bilberry covered ledge. Head up and right on to easy ground to finish.
FA. Z.Leppert, M.Kellas 1988

❷ Broadsword E2 5c

The best route on the crag and a great and powerful adventure. Start at the perched block on the low ledge down and right of the hanging quartzy-ramp.
1) 5c, 25m. Climb the wall to gain a hand traverse leftwards on to the sloping quartzy-ramp. Climb the corner above and surmount the capping overhang to gain a belay.
2) 5c, 12m. Climb the delicate pocketed arete above the belay.
3) 5b, 12m. Power up the steep crack above to reach the ledge.
FA. Z.Leppert, M.Kellas 1988

❸ Gawain Direct E2 5c

A good route and well worth seeking out..
1) 5c, 18m. Climb the overhanging corner, passing a heathery ledge, to gain the quartz ramp. Follow this leftwards to belay near the mossy groove.
2) 5a, 14m. Climb the mossy groove and then zig zag up grassy ground to reach a belay beneath the good diagonal corner above.
3) 5c, 18m. Follow the diagonal corner above to reach a good ledge.
4) 5b, 12m. As for pitch 3 of *Broadsword*.
FA. D.Alcock, C.Davies (2pts) 1969

❹ Gwynhyfryd E4 6b

Remember kids - E4's are hard!
1) 6b, 25m. Cut a path up the knife-edged arete and squirm your way on to the sloping ledge on the right. Make a committing move up the rounded arete above to gain the belay.
2) 4a, 10m. Trend up and diagonally left to reach a good belay.
3) 5c, 25m. Climb the steep crack above to gain easier ground.
FA. Z.Leppert, P.Holden 1990

❺ Cadwaladr E3 6a

A nice crackline that is steeper than it first appears. Best climbed in very dry conditions as the start stays wet. Start a few metres right of the arete below the prominent crack.
1) 6a, 28m. Surmount the overlap (often damp) and reach the crack. Follow this (more strenuous than it looks) to a junction with the arete. Step right and climb the wall.
2) 4b, 32m. Climb the slab and continuation groove to finish, various options.
FA. Z.Leppart, W.Barker 1989

Betws y Coed

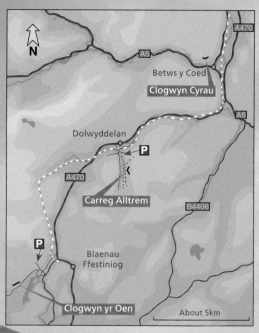

Tremadog

Cwm Silyn

Cloggy

Llanberis

Lliwedd

Ogwen

Carneddau

Betws y Coed

Welsh Winter

N

A470

A5

Betws y Coed

Clogwyn Cyrau

A5

Dolwyddelan

P

A470

Carreg Alltrem

B4406

P

Blaenau
Ffestiniog

Clogwyn yr Oen

About 5km

Alan James high on *Fratricide Wall* (HVS) - *page 174* - at Carreg Alltrem. Photo: Mick Ryan

Tremadog

Cwm Silyn

Cloggy

Llanberis

Lliwedd

Ogwen

Carneddau

Betws y Coed

Welsh Winter

Tremadog | Cwm Silyn | Cloggy | Llanberis | Lliwedd | Ogwen | Carneddau | Betws y Coed | Welsh Winter

Clogwyn Cyrau

Set in the trees above the bustling village of Betws y Coed, the Cyrau crags offer some nice short climbs with a lovely view over the valley. The Little Buttress is perfect for single-pitch group use and is an easy place to set up top-ropes - an ideal place to introduce beginners.

The Main Buttress has some longer and very worthwhile routes. Whilst not up to the mountain magnificence of Cloggy, they are a sunny alternative for those based near Betws and might help you escape those tea shops!

Approach - From the pay and display carpark, follow the road parallel to the river, walking upstream, take the first right turn and follow that road as it turns in to a private Forestry Commission road. Follow this as it U-turns back leftwards underneath some wooden Alpine-esque houses (way marker sign post on the left bend). The road then turns into a track and there is a footpath on the right (see photo).

For Little Buttress - Turn right (marked Cyrau, white footprint) after 20m. Pass under some buttresses and take a steep path leading leftwards to the Little Buttress.

For Main Crag - Follow the road (marked Pen yr Allt, blue footprint) up the hill until a vague path leads rightwards along an old wall to the base of the cliff.

Approach

Little Buttress

A great single pitch venue. There are many more worthwhile low-grade routes around to the left of this front face.

GPS 53.094370 -3.806000

About 500m

① **Direct Route** . . . 🏔① ☐ **VS 4c**
A nice route up the clean pocketed wall.
12m. Start at the left side of the square overhang and climb directly up the wall to gain a groove near the top.

② **Eliminate Start** . 🖼 ☐ **VS 5a**
A nice right-hand variation to *Direct Route*.
12m. Start at the right side of the small square overhang and follow cracks to the ledge, then join *Direct Route*.

③ **Pryderi** . . . . 🏔 🖼 ☐ **VS 4c**
A pleasant technical challenge.
12m. From just left of the block on the floor climb straight up to follow a vague crackline.

④ **Gwyndion** . . . . ☐ **VS 4c**
The rightmost of the worthwhile routes.
11m. Start on top of the block and climb the wall to gain a groove on the left to finish.

Little Buttress **Clogwyn Cyrau**

Lots of sun | 20 min | Sheltered

Descent

Plenty more
good easier
routes for
beginners

1

2

3

4

Tremadog

Cwm Silyn

Cloggy

Llanberis

Lliwedd

Ogwen

Carneddau

Betws y Coed

Welsh Winter

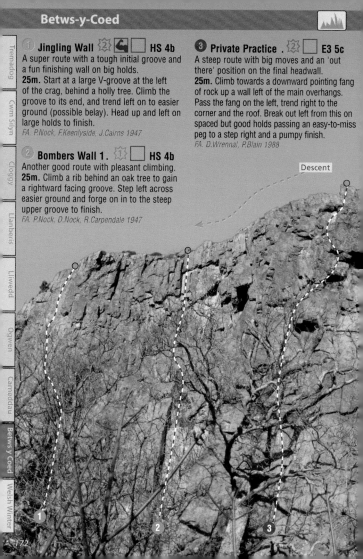

① Jingling Wall   HS 4b

A super route with a tough initial groove and a fun finishing wall on big holds.
25m. Start at a large V-groove at the left of the crag, behind a holly tree. Climb the groove to its end, and trend left on to easier ground (possible belay). Head up and left on large holds to finish.
FA. P.Nock, F.Keenlyside, J.Cairns 1947

② Bombers Wall 1.   HS 4b

Another good route with pleasant climbing.
25m. Climb a rib behind an oak tree to gain a rightward facing groove. Step left across easier ground and forge on in to the steep upper groove to finish.
FA. P.Nock, D.Nock, R.Carpendale 1947

❸ Private Practice .   E3 5c

A steep route with big moves and an 'out there' position on the final headwall.
25m. Climb towards a downward pointing fang of rock up a wall left of the main overhangs. Pass the fang on the left, trend right to the corner and the roof. Break out left from this on spaced but good holds passing an easy-to-miss peg to a step right and a pumpy finish.
FA. D.Wrennal, P.Blain 1988

Descent

Tremadog

Cwm Silyn

Cloggy

Llanberis

Lliwedd

Ogwen

Carneddau

Betws-y-Coed

Welsh Winter

1   2   3

④ Hywel Dda . . . . . ⚄ ☐ E2 5b

Start just right of the main overhangs beneath a long ledge at 6m.

25m. Climb to the ledge and continue keeping a broken crack system on your left. At 15m don't take an easy option rightwards, but pull steeply up on jugs and traverse right between the overhangs.

FA. P.Littlejohn, P.Judge 1991

⑤ Long Climb Direct

. . . . ⚄ 🖼️ ☐ S

A good route with nice moves that offers an amenable way up the main cliff.

25m. Start behind at oak tree. Follow rock steps rightwards and gain a ledge right of a rib. Continue awkwardly up the corner and gain a rounded spike. Traverse left, pass a small tree and head back right to a ledge. Climb the corner to the top.

FA. D.Wrennal, R.Mulliss 1983

⑥ Central Route 2 . ⚄ ☐ VS 4c

A very good and direct line.

25m. Start as for the previous route. Gain the ledge and climb the broad rib above to a niche at 12m. Step left round a blunt rib and gain a ledge, and fight up the short corner right of a bulge to follow a groove to the top.

Main Cliff

Some good, long single-pitch routes that pack a punch. The central section sports a steep headwall and some pumpy climbing, whilst the slightly less steep side-walls have more to offer the technical climber.

Tremadog

Cwm Silyn

Cloggy

Llanberis

Lliwedd

Ogwen

Carneddau

Betws y Coed

Welsh Winter

Tremadog | Cwm Silyn | Cloggy | Llanberis | Lliwedd | Ogwen | Carneddau | Betws y Coed | Welsh Winter

Carreg Alltrem

This delightful small crag is easy to miss when faced with the more concentrated hotspots of The Pass, Ogwen and Tremadog. It has the added bonus of being relatively sheltered with a pleasant west-facing aspect, getting the afternoon sun.

Approach - From the main road in the middle of Dolwyddelan, turn south towards the railway station, cross the river and the railway and follow the road around to the left. Park carefully in the gateway. A wide track leads up through the woods, to the crag.

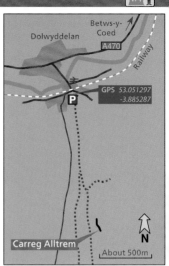

GPS 53.051297 -3.885287

Carreg Alltrem

About 500m

N

1 Fratricide Wall

. . . . 🔅 ▨ ☐ **HVS 5a**

This long and intricate route weaves a complex line up a steep wall. The climbing is sustained with plenty of hard moves interspersed with good rests but it is thin on gear. High in the grade. *Photo on page 168.*

1) 4c, 21m. Climb a steep crack to a ledge. Follow the slim groove above then easier ground back leftwards to a good stance.

2) 5a, 23m. A complex pitch. Climb a steep crack and wall to good ledges. Balance precariously right then pull up to the base of a scoop. Climb the groove above to a peg, then swing right to the arete.

FA. C.Jones, A.Jones, A.Daffern (1 pt) 1960

2 Lightning Visit . . 🔅 ☐ **VS 4c**

The second of the trio of classics follows the wall and slim groove in the centre of the crag. The one to start on to get yourself warmed up.

1) 4a, 17m. Climb a cracked groove and then follow blocky ledges up above to a good stance.

2) 4c, 20m. Move up and right to gain the groove proper. After some tricky moves this leads more easily to the top and a finish on the left.

FA. R.James, C.Jones 1959

3 Lavaredo . . . . . 🔅 ☐ **VS 5a**

The final classic in the trio and the best. The first pitch is nicely intricate and the second is a stupendous jug-haul in a situation normally reserved for routes around three grades harder.

1) 4b, 20m. Climb the slim groove to its top, then pull slightly right onto the steep wall which leads to a large grassy ledge.

2) 5a, 23m. Pull up leftwards on some good spike holds. Arrange gear then make a long move to more good holds. Hang on here to get some gear in, or move quickly up and right if you are tired, where the gear is easier to place. Climb up and then left on magnificent holds to finish up a corner. The grade of VS 5a is a little deceptive and those with long arms will probably find it easier than 5a, and those who tire quickly on steep ground may find it harder than VS!

FA. R.James, K.Forder, I.Campbell 1961

Descent is down
a very steep gully
50m to the right,
or abseil from
fixed slings

A

Civetta (E3)

Penammen Groove (E1)

1

2

3

Tremadog

Cwm Silyn

Cloggy

Llanberis

Lliwedd

Ogwen

Carneddau

Betws y Coed

Welsh Winter

① Kirkus's Climb Direct ⚐⚐ ☐ S 4a

A great route that picks its way up the nose of the crag on steep sections of clean rock.

1) 4a, 18m. Start at the toe of the rib, climb the short steep wall to gain the top of the pinnacle. Move right to a cave/block belay.

2) 4a, 12m. Make steep moves right to gain the slab which is followed to a good ledge.

3) 4a, 20m. Climb the slabby groove then the slab on the right after a ledge.

4) 12m. Climb the right hand groove to easier ground and good belays well back.

FA. C.F.Kirkus, C.G.Kirkus 1928

② Chic . . . . ⚐ ☐ VDiff

A good easy-angled line with nice situations.

1) 25m. Climb the prominent rib to a ledge.

2) 22m. Swing up the steep wall to a ledge, step left and gain the left edge of the slab. Climb up and right to a long ledge.

3) 18m. Climb the rightward leaning crack, pad up the slab to a ledge then pull over the short corner above to finish.

FA. A.Moulam, W.Craster, C.Brasher 1952

Pinky (VS 4c)

Descent

Clogwyn yr Oen

This delightful multi-pitch crag has many great mid-grade routes, most of which have ample belay stances and fun, technical sections on clean rock.

Descent - Follow a terrace along the top of the crag leftwards to gain a small path that leads down an open gully down the left side of the crag

Tremadog

Cwm Silyn

Cloggy

Llanberis

Lliwedd

Ogwen

Carneddau

Betws y Coed

Welsh Winter

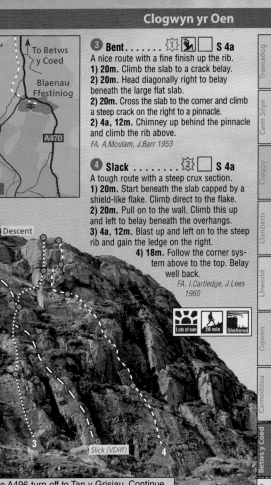

❸ Bent . . . . 🏕 🧗 ▢ S 4a

A nice route with a fine finish up the rib.
1) 20m. Climb the slab to a crack belay.
2) 20m. Head diagonally right to belay beneath the large flat slab.
2) 20m. Cross the slab to the corner and climb a steep crack on the right to a pinnacle.
2) 4a, 12m. Chimney up behind the pinnacle and climb the rib above.
FA. A.Moulam, J.Barr 1953

❹ Slack . . . . 🏕 ▢ S 4a

A tough route with a steep crux section.
1) 20m. Start beneath the slab capped by a shield-like flake. Climb direct to the flake.
2) 20m. Pull on to the wall. Climb this up and left to belay beneath the overhangs.
3) 4a, 12m. Blast up and left on to the steep rib and gain the ledge on the right.
4) 18m. Follow the corner system above to the top. Belay well back.
FA. I.Cartledge, J.Lees 1960

Lots of sun | 20 min | Sheltered

Approach - From the A496 turn off to Tan y Grisiau. Continue up the narrow steep road to its end and parking by a gate and the quarry entrance. Follow a path up and left over a footbridge across the stream to join the private access tarmac road. Walk up the road for 1km until you are directly under the crag.

Welsh Winter

Tremadog
Cwm Silyn
Cloggy
Llanberis
Lliwedd
Ogwen
Carneddau
Betwys Coed
Welsh Winter

Perfect ice in Cwm Idwal. A climber tackles *The Curtain* (IV) and in the background another sets off up *The Screen* (IV) - *page 193*. Photo: Jack Geldard

Tremadog

Cwm Silyn

Cloggy

Llanberis

Lliwedd

Ogwen

Carneddau

Betws y Coed

Welsh Winter

Tremadog | Cwm Silyn | Cloggy | Llanberis | Lliwedd | Ogwen | Carneddau | Betws y Coed | Welsh Winter

Covered in the Llanberis Winter section is the giant mountainside of the Trinity Face on Snowdon, a superb set of snow gullies and long mountaineering routes. These are the highest winter routes in Wales and are climbed most winters.

Juxtaposed against the easy-angled gullies of the Trinity Face are a set of super-steep ice routes on the shady side of The Pass. Cascade and Central Icefall Direct are essential winter ticks for anyone who loves vertical ice.

Conditions

The Trinity Face gullies get climbed in a range of conditions, and are one of the first places to get snow cover. The harder and more consolidated the snow, the better.

Craig y Rhaeadr freezes only in the coldest of winters and it is easily possible to check the condition of the icefalls from the Llanberis Pass road. *Cascade* is one of the first to form, usually very thinly, whilst the icicle pitch of *Central Icefall Direct* is rarely climbable. Obviously the routes are harder and more serious in thin or thaw conditions, which is how you are most likely to find them.

James McHaffie climbing a thin first pitch of *Cascade* (V) - *page 183*. The line of *Cascade Right-hand* (V) is clearly visible on the right. Photo: Jack Geldard

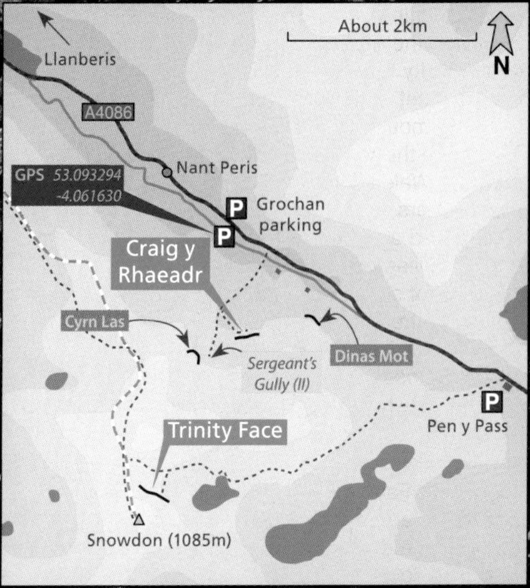

About 2km

N

Llanberis

A4086

GPS 53.093294
-4.061630

Nant Peris

P
P Grochan
parking

Craig y
Rhaeadr

Cyrn Las

Sergeant's
Gully (II)

Dinas Mot

Trinity Face

P
Pen y Pass

Snowdon (1085m)

Approach *see also page 108 for approach to Pen y Pass*

Trinity Face - From the car park at Pen y Pass (busy!)
head up the miners track to reach the large lake of
Llyn Llydaw and follow the track as it contours round
the right side of the lake. As the Miners track rears up
for its final slog to the top of the col, the Trinity Face is
on your left.

Craig y Rhaeadr (Cascade) - Park in one of the
laybys below the Grochan. Cross the bridge and head
up the hillside on a small track on the right side of
the stream (as for Cyrn Las on page 106). Halfway
up the hill break left and contour across to reach the
foot of the crag. The stream that you have followed
cuts up the hillside to the left of Cyrn Las and where it
steepens up it becomes a superb set of ice steps and
is *Sergeant's Gully* a nice grade 2.

Tremadog

Cwm Silyn

Clogwy

Llanberis

Lliwedd

Ogwen

Carneddau

Glaew y Coed

Walsh Winter

181

Descent ---→

Craig y Rhaeadr

The infamous icefalls of Craig y Rhaeadr are steep, committing and usually in thin condition. *Central Icefall Direct* is the last to form, and is the most sought after winter prize in Wales.

Approach - From the approach for Cyrn Las, break left halfway up the hill and contour across to reach the crag. See map on page 181.

Descent - The descent from the crag is well over to the right (looking in).

Waterfall Climb (IV,5)

Tremadog
Cwm Silyn
Cloggy
Llanberis
Lliwedd
Ogwen
Carneddau
Betws y Coed
Welsh Winter

Not much sun — 30 min

1 Chequered Wall VI,6

A steep and rarely-formed route, but one that can give an alternative finish to *Central Icefall Direct* when the icicle hasn't touched down.
1) 5, 35m. Climb the steep left-hand icefall to a ledge on the right on top of the pedestal.
2) 6, 40m. Move left to regain the icefall. Climb this, belay on the right under the overhangs.
3) 6, 30m. Skirt the overhang on the left, then head diagonally back right above. Continue as far as the rope will allow to belay well back.

2 Central Icefall Direct VI,6

The one route that everyone wants to do. If it is in condition (rarely) then get up early and get ready to queue. Worth the wait though!
1) 5, 30m. Climb the icefall on the front of the pedestal to a ledge belay.
2) 6, 40m. A long, pumpy pitch up the steep icefall above leads to a belay either left or right of the icicle, depending on conditions.
3) 6, 30m. Tackle the overhanging icicle direct!
3a) 6, 35m. If the icicle hasn't formed thick enough for your mate to lead it, you can sneak left to join *Chequered Wall*, which is sometimes 'in nick' when the main icicle isn't.

The weaving route of **Waterfall Climb** *finds a way up the cliff at a grade of* **IV,5** *but is virtually as tricky as the main event routes, and is only really worthwhile if you have either done everything else, or really can't tackle* Cascade.

3 Cascade V,5

This sweep of perfect ice gives a great and sustained outing and is often high in the grade. *Photo on page 180.*
1) 5, 50m. Climb the icefall, sometimes passing a rock runner at 10m on the right, to gain a ledge (possible belay). Climb the short steep wall above to another ledge.
2) 5, 60m. Move left from the belay (old pegs) and pump rightwards across steep ice to gain the more slabby wall above. Follow this direct and belay as far back as possible.

4 Cascade Right-hand V,5

A rarely formed variation to *Cascade*, but worth of a mention as the upper section may enable you to avoid a queue on the parent route.
1) 5, 50m. Climb an ice gully just right of *Cascade*.
2) 5, 60m. Follow the icefall above, keeping to the right. Belay well back.

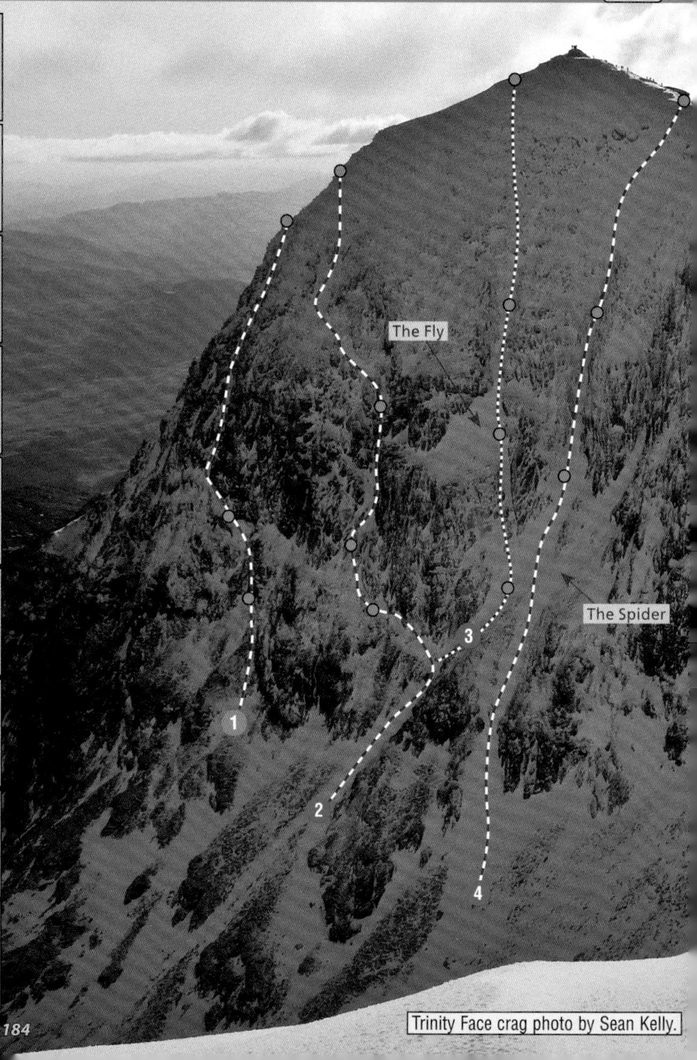

Tremadog

Cwm Silyn

Cloggy

Llanberis

Lliwedd

Ogwen

Carneddau

Betws-y-Coed

Welsh Winter

The Fly

The Spider

1

2

3

4

Trinity Face crag photo by Sean Kelly.

Tremadog

Cwm Silyn

Cloggy

Llanberis

Lliwedd

Ogwen

Carneddau

Betws y Coed

Welsh Winter

Descent

Trinity Face

The bastion of Welsh winter gully climbing, The Trinity Face is often in condition. The routes top-out on the summit of Snowdon, giving amazing views of Snowdonia.

Approach - See map on page 181.
Descent - Descend the ridge right-wards to drop down the main path returning to the base of the routes.

Not much sun · 55 min

① Great Gully III,3

The prominent gully on the far left of the crag gives a good and varied route.
1) 3, 60m. Climb the gully, passing various chockstones (dependant on snow level) to belay in an easier-angled bowl of snow.
2) 3, 30m. Climb the short icefall in the continuation gully (can be passed on the left at Grade II) and continue into the gully up and left.
3) 1, 140m. The long snow-gully leads to the top. Various belay options exist.

② Little Gully. . . . . II/III

Another good route that is best done in firm snow-conditions.
1) 1, 100m. Follow the large snow gully to a ledge system leading left. Follow the ledge leftwards for 50m until beneath the icy gully.
2) 2, 20m. Follow the gully to beneath the prominent steep corner.
3) 3, 60m. Follow the difficult iced-up corner to reach easier broken ground and a belay.
4) 1, 100m. The easy snow-slope leads to the ridge.

③ Left-hand Trinity I/II

A good, long snow route that gives a classic winter-outing.
1) 1, 100m. Climb the easy snow-ramp to the snow patch called The Spider.
2) 1, 60m. Follow the icy gully leftwards to gain The Fly.
3) 2, 50m. Exit The Fly by the gully at its apex.
4) 1, 110m. Follow the easy snow slope to finish just left of the summit.

④ Central Trinity . . I/II

THE classic low-grade winter route in Wales. Long, atmospheric and involved, this route gives a great mountain adventure and in good, firm snow is a great choice for first steps in winter.
1) 1, 130m. The broad central gully leads directly to The Spider.
2) 1/2, 60m. The gully at the top left corner of The Spider passes some nice icy steps.
3) 1, 110m. Continue up the slope to gain the ridge right of the summit.

① Trinity Buttress . . . . 🗲📷☐ III,3

A short, but worthwhile section of interesting climbing that is a good choice if the other routes on the face are busy with climbers, which is a regular occurrence in good conditions!

1) 1, 130m. Climb the easy snow-ramp to the snow patch called The Spider.
2) 3, 50m. Climb rightwards up the gully until it steepens. Break left to reach a snow field.
3) 2, 100m. Follow the final snow-slope to the summit.

② Right-hand Trinity . . . . 🗲☐ II/III

The right-hand finish of the classic Trinity gullies gives another great snow route.

1) 1, 130m. Climb the easy snow-ramp to the snow patch called The Spider.
2) 2, 30m. Follow the gully rightwards until the walls become more pronounced.
3) 3, 40m. Continue up the gully with interest.
4) 3, 50m. More tricky icy-gully climbing.
5) 1, 100m. The easy snow-slope leads to the summit.

③ Laddie's Gully . . . . 🗲☐ III,3

One for the boys? This route is good, but slightly inferior to *Ladies' Gully*.

1) 3, 40m. Climb the left-hand of the twin gullies at the top of a snow patch.
2) 3, 40m. Continue up the gully to reach a terrace.
3) 3, 100m. Trend right over mixed ground to reach a gully heading up and left. Climb this onto the much easier final snow slopes which are followed to the summit.

④ Ladies' Gully . . . . 🗲🧗☐ III,3

The parallel line to *Laddie's Gully* is another great outing with wonderful climbing.

1) 2, 60m. Follow the stepped gully past some interesting pulls to a belay where it steepens.
2) 3, 25m. The steep section gives a great ice-pitch with a stiff pull to finish.
3) 1, 110m. Continue up the gully and snow slope to gain the ridge, well right of the summit.

⑤ Cave Gully . . . . 🗲🧗☐ III,4

A brilliant route, but one that can have a problematic middle pitch in soft snow conditions.

1) 2, 45m. Follow the deep gully to a belay beneath an overhang.
2) 4, 20m. Battle past the overhang via a steep groove on the left and continue to a cave.
3) 2, 60m. Climb leftwards from the cave belay to gain easier ground and the ridge.

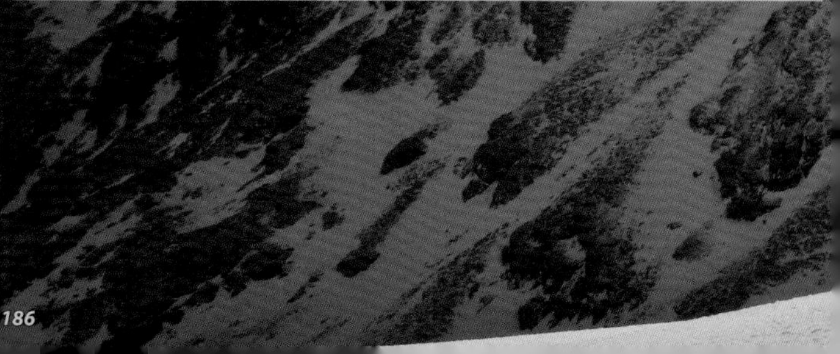

Side tabs (vertical): Tremadog · Cwm Silyn · Cloggy · Llanberis · Llwedd · Ogwen · Carneddau · Betws y Coed · Welsh Winter

Not much sun

55 min

Descent

The Spider

2

1

3 4

5

Tremadog

Cwm Silyn

Clogwyn

Llanberis

Lliwedd

Ogwen

Carneddau

Betws y Coed

Welsh Winter

The Icefalls of Cwm Idwal are easily accessible, great fun and short enough to do a few in a day. There are steep desperate routes such as the *Devil's Appendix* and some mid grade classics like *South Gully* and *The Screen*. Alll are superb quality routes and can get very busy when conditions are good. The atmosphere on the short ice-pitch of *The Devil's Kitchen* is second to none and this whole area is a wonderful winter playground.

Approach

Park at Ogwen Cottage on the A5 and follow the main path up into Cwm Idwal. Pass under the Idwal Slabs and continue along the track up in to the back of the Cwm. Cross the stream (this stream can be climbed higher up as a superb series of ice steps and is called simply *The Idwal Stream*, grade 2) and make a break up to the cliffs.

Conditions

A good freeze is needed for these ice routes to form. The most reliable are *The Ramp* and *The Screen* and *South Gully*. The hanging icicle of *The Devil's Appendix* rarely forms thickly enough to be climbed, but if it does start to freeze up, don't break it off before it touches down!

Descent

South Gully and Devil's Pipes

Screen Area

GPS 53.125213 -3.984070

To Bethesda

A5

Ogwen Cottage

P

P

P

To Capel Curig

Gwern Gof Uchaf

Sting

Devil's Appendix

South Gully

Clogwyn Du

N

About 1km

The Devil's Kitchen

Devil's Appendix and The Sting

1 South Gully . . . . 3 ☒ IV,4
A superb ice-gully that cuts an obvious swathe down the far left of the crag.
1) 3, 35m. Climb the initial icefall to a good ledge and belay on the right of the gully.
2) 4, 45m. The big central pitch can be climbed on the left at Grade 4 or directly up the right side at Grade 5. Exit slightly right onto easier ground and a good belay.
3) 2, 30m. Climb the easier top pitch passing one ice bulge to belay as far back as possible.

2 Central Route . . . . ☒ III,4
A good route when fully formed, but more difficult in soft snow.
1) 4, 30m. Climb the second ice gully right of *South Gully* to an ease in angle.
2) 3, 45m. Continue up the gully, gradually easing, to a left slanting gangway.
3) 1, 45m. Follow the gangway easily leftwards to a scramble finish.

3 Grecian 2000 . . . . 11 IV,5
A good route and high in the grade. The top pitch has a formidable reputation.
1) 5, 50m. Climb the hanging icicle on the left of the gully to belay on the ramp.
2) 1, 25m. Easily up the ramp to a belay below the steep icy corner.
3) 5, 35m. Follow the line of ice to the roof. Pull right into a corner and follow it to the top.

④ Chicane Gully . . . . 🏔2 ☐ III,4
Another good route, when in condition. The second pitch can be very hard in unconsolidated snow.
1) 3, 45m. Climb the icy groove right of the icicle until more ice leads back leftwards into the main gully. Follow this to easier ground on the ramp.
2) 4, 45m. Move right to gain the continuation gully. Follow this to an ease in angle.
3) 1, 30m. Easy angled ground leads to the top. Belay well back.

⑤ Devil's Pipes . . . . 🏔3 🗺️ 🪓 ☐ V,6
A fantastic icy outing that is both bold and steep.
1) 4, 40m. Start just left of the toe of the buttress and climb stepped ice.
2) 6, 60m. Climb directly up the steep icefall. (Belay possible at half height).

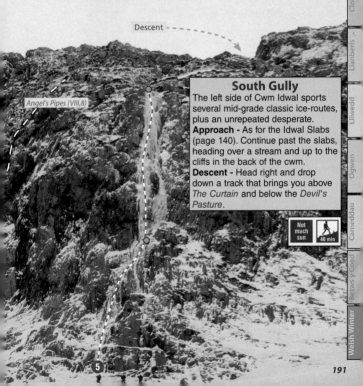

Descent ⤏

Angel's Pipes (VIII,8)

South Gully
The left side of Cwm Idwal sports several mid-grade classic ice-routes, plus an unrepeated desperate.
Approach - As for the Idwal Slabs (page 140). Continue past the slabs, heading over a stream and up to the cliffs in the back of the cwm.
Descent - Head right and drop down a track that brings you above *The Curtain* and below the *Devil's Pasture*.

Not much sun | 40 min

Tremadog · Cwm Silyn · Cloggy · Llanberis · Lliwedd · Ogwen · Carneddau · Betws y Coed · Welsh Winter

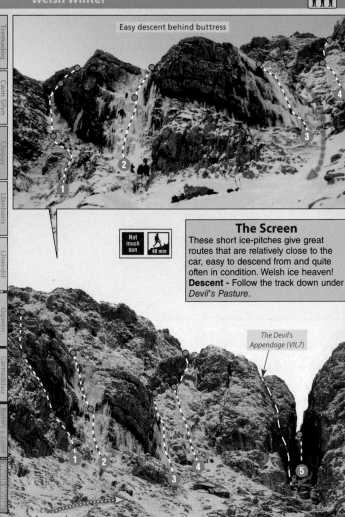

Easy descent behind buttress

1

2

3

4

Not much sun

40 min

The Screen

These short ice-pitches give great routes that are relatively close to the car, easy to descend from and quite often in condition. Welsh ice heaven!

Descent - Follow the track down under *Devil's Pasture*.

The Devil's Appendage (VII,7)

1

2

3

4

5

Approach

Tremadog | Cwm Silyn | Clogwy | Llanberis | Lliwedd | Ogwen | Carneddau | Betws y Coed | Welsh Winter

❶ The Ramp III,3
The leftmost ice ramp gives a fine route.
1) 2, 25m. A short icy pitch leads leftwards to
the foot of the ramp proper.
2) 3, 40m. Blast up the ramp, turning a steep
section where the ice swings right.
2) 1, 25m. An easy snow-gully remains.

❷ The Screen IV,4
Another great ice-route. *Photo on page 178.*
1) 3, 20m. Climb the large ice-wall to a ledge
belay beneath steeper ice.
2) 4, 45m. Pull over the steep ice above and
continue up the easier angled flow. Exit right or
left depending on conditions.

❸ The Curtain IV,4
This short route is steep and packs a punch.
1) 4, 30m. Climb the steep ice-pitch just left of
the descent track. The pitch is sometimes started
on the right. A good belay is found well back on
a huge boulder.
Photo on page 178.

❹ Devil's Pasture . III,3
The superb icy route has a wonderful first pitch
and a great chimney to finish.
Photo this page.
1) 3, 30m. Climb the river of ice, wherever it
has formed best, to belay beneath the chimney
on the left.
2) 3, 45m. The chimney leads to an easy gully.

*On the left side of the deep gully, sometimes
hangs the icicle of* **The Devil's Appendage VII,7**.

❺ The Devil's Kitchen IV,4
Perhaps the most atmospheric ice-route in
Wales. Scramble all the way up the deep cleft
until you reach the waterfall.
30m. Climb the icefall on the right of the waterfall. Belay well back.

Perfect ice on the first pitch of *Devil's Pasture* (III,3) - *this page*. Photo: Jack Geldard

Tremadog Cwm Silyn Cloggy Llanberis Lliwedd Ogwen Carneddau Betws y Coed Welsh Winter

Welsh Winter

Tremadog
Cwm Silyn
Cloggy
Llanberis
Lliwedd
Ogwen
Carneddau
Betws y Coed
Welsh Winter

Not much sun 40 min

1 **Devil's Staircase** V,6
A great mixed route tackling the impending chimney-line left of *The Devil's Appendix*.
1) 6, 25m. Climb the technical and sometimes thinly-iced chimney.
2) 5, 15m. Either attack the chockstone-chimney above or skirt it on the left via an icy wall.
3) 4, 20m. A snow slope leads to a steeper groove with a tricky pull.
4) 5, 40m. Gain the final chimney on the right and squirm up this to glory.

2 **The Devil's Appendix** VI,6
The steep icicle of *The Devil's Appendix* gives a fantastic strenuous pitch followed by an
equally exciting top pitch of great character, passing some amazing ice formations.
1) 6, 30m. Climb the icefall to beneath the roof and hanging icicle (pegs on the left). Launch
on to the hanging icicle praying that it doesn't collapse. Climb the steep wall above to the
ledge and a loose-ish blocky belay stance. The icicle can sometimes be avoided on the left if
it hasn't formed enough to be climbed.
2) 5, 60m. Climb the ice, first rightwards to a ledge, then back left into a corner (possible
cramped belay). Traverse right to the far-right of the icefall and finish direct.

Approach for *Devil's Appendix*

194

Tremadog
Cwm Silyn
Cloggy
Llanberis
Lliwedd
Ogwen
Carneddau
Betws y Coed
Welsh Winter

The Devil's Appendix

The right side of Cwm Idwal has one of the most sought after ice routes in Wales.
Approach - *Devil's Staircase* and *The Devil's Appendix* are approached along a high level path from the base of the deep cleft below the *Devil's Kitchen* (shown on topo). The routes on the right are approached along the base of the cliffs.
Descent - A descent can be made down the Goat Track (shown) or by walking left to reach the track down near *Devil's Pasture* (shown on previous page).

❸ **The Devil's Filthbag** . . . . 🕮2 ✂️🎿 ☐ **V,5**
The left-most ice line gives a thrilling, if short pitch.
1) 5, 45m. Climb the steep icefall and belay on the ramp.

❹ **The Sting** . . . . 🕮2 🧗 ☐ **V,5**
Another classic Idwal icefall with a wonderfully exposed second pitch.
1) 3, 10m. Climb the initial icefall to a cave belay on the left.
2) 5, 45m. Step back right onto the ice pillar and climb it direct to a rightward leaning groove. Follow this to the ramp and belay well back.

❺ **The Devil's Cellar** . . . . 🕮 ✂️🎿🐚 ☐ **IV,5**
Another enjoyable ice-climb that is a good bet if the *South Gully* area is busy.
1) 4, 30m. Climb the wall of ice or the groove on the left to a poor belay on a ramp.
2) 5, 40m. Move right and follow the steep line of ice to gain the top of the descent ramp.

Descent

❶ Cracking Up . ⊕⟨3⟩ 🗺 ☐ IX,9
A steep and scary route.
1) 4, 12m. Climb up onto the large spike.
2) 9, 55m. Climb the steep, pumpy crack!

❷ Travesty. ⟨2⟩ 🗺 🔧 ☐ VIII,8
Another bold and desperate route.
1) 4, 12m. As for *Cracking Up.*
2) 8, 12m. Traverse desperately up and right to gain the sanctuary of the slanting gully.
3) 5, 40m. Continue up the gully passing a short and tricky chimney section.

❸ Pillar Chimney . . ⟨3⟩ ☐ V,6
A classic winter outing. If the chimney is devoid of ice it can be skirted to the right.
1) 3, 50m. Climb the long slanting gully and belay at the base of the chimney/pillar.
2) 6, 15m. Climb the steep chimney, the more ice the better, to a chockstone belay.
3) 4, 25m. An icy wall leads to a leftward slanting slab.

❹ Blender Head ⟨2⟩ 🔧 ☐ VII,8
A tough but well-protected route.
1) 3, 30m. *Pillar Chimney* to a thread belay.
2) 4, 15m. Climb left across the slab to a ledge beneath a groove.
3) 8, 25m. Climb the desperately pumpy groove then traverse left to gain *Travesty.*
4) 5, 28m. Finish up *Travesty.*

❺ El Mancho . . ⟨3⟩ 🔧 ☐ VII,7
A neo-classic mixed climb with a grand finale.
1) 3, 50m. As for *Pillar Chimney.*
2) 5, 20m. Climb down the ramp for 3 metres and access a turf covered ledge system. Shuffle along this to a good belay.
3) 7, 35m. Balance into the groove above to gain a small ledge. Climb the crack to a roof, pull left to a ledge and follow the cracked wall above.

Just right again is **Manx Wall, VI,6** *which follows the original summer HS.*

❻ Left-hand Branch ⟨3⟩ ☐ IV,5
A classic route with a tough and steep second pitch. The more ice the better.
1) 2, 30m. Follow the gully until it closes in. Belay below an icy left-wall.
2) 5, 30m. The chimney is overcome by strenuous bridging and then a step onto the left wall proper. Climb this to a good belay.
3) 3, 35m. Climb over the large chockstone and belay beneath the final exit chimney.
4) 3, 30m. Climb the chimney and a steep snow slope to finish. Belay well back.

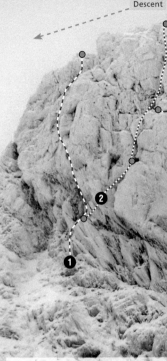

Clogwyn Du

This short but steep mixed venue offers fine technical climbing that comes into condition fairly regularly.
Approach - Climb the slope directly up from the cwm.
Descent - Descend easily, well off to the left of the crag.

Route climbs behind pillar

Manx Wall VI,6

Mixed alternative

A V,5 variation links LH to RH

7 **Right-hand Branch** ⚒️ ☐ **III,3**
A great route with contrasting sections.
1) 3, 55m. From the right-hand side of the snow fan, head up and right through icy ground to belay on easy angled ground at the base of the upper gully.
2) 3, 45m. Climb the chimney above, pass a jammed boulder and step right to belay beneath the continuation gully.
3) 3, 15m. Climb the final gully and surmount a chockstone at the very top. Belay well back.

Clogwyn Du crag photo by Pierre Maxtad.

Tremadog | Cwm Silyn | Cloggy | Llanberis | Lliwedd | Ogwen | Carneddau | Betws y Coed | Welsh Winter

The huge vegetated north-facing cliff of the Black Ladders is Wales' biggest and baddest winter climbing ground. The cliffs are home to several classic gullies and ice lines as well as a host of modern mixed climbs. Be prepared for long routes, cold conditions, big days out and a real adventure. Welcome to Wales!

Approach

From the A5 take the Braichmelyn road up into the village and park your car sensibly in Gerlan, Bethesda. Follow the Gerlan road rightwards leading towards the waterworks to reach the waterworks. Cross a stile on the right of the waterworks to gain a broad valley which is followed via a path on the right side of the stream leading along the valley and finally arriving at the cliff, about an hour from the car.

Descent

Follow the summit plateau leftwards and drop back into the valley well to the left of *Eastern Gully*, down the easy hillside.

Eastern Gully   Central Gully   Western Gully (V,6) - page 202

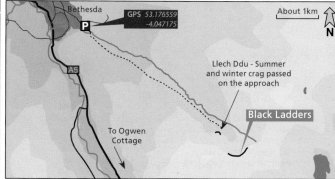

Bethesda

GPS 53.176559 -4.047175

About 1km

N

Llech Ddu - Summer and winter crag passed on the approach

Black Ladders

A5

To Ogwen Cottage

Tremadog | Cwm Silyn | Cloggy | Llanberis | Lliwedd | Ogwen | Carneddau | Betws y Coed | Welsh Winter

Tremadog · Cwm Silyn · Cloggy · Llanberis · Lliwedd · Ogwen · Carneddau · Berwyn & Coed · Welsh Winter

① Eastern Gully . . . 2 ☐ III,3

The deep gully on the far left of the crag.
1) 3, 45m. A steep icefall-start gives access to the gully proper. An easier start from the right is possible if the ice hasn't formed.
2) 1, 65m. Follow the easy central gully.
3) 2, 90m. Take the steeper right-hand finish.

② Pyramid Gully . . 2 ☐ IV,5

Another classic gully climb with some excellent ice on the first two pitches.
1) 5, 45m. Climb the steep ice-pitch to the snow ledge and belay on the left.
2) 4, 35m. Climb the icefall to the easing in angle, exit right onto the snow slope.
3) 1, 120m. Easily up the snow to finish.

Descent

Not much sun — 80 min

③ Pyramid Face Direct
☐ V,6

A technical winter-excursion with a fine icefall first-pitch and a mixed middle.
1) 5, 45m. Climb the wide icefall to reach a large ledge-system on the left.
2) 6, 80m. Traverse left to gain a steep system of grooves. Follow these directly for 80m, several belay possibilites available.
3) 4, 60m. Continue up easier mixed ground to reach the summit.

④ Central Gully 2 ☐ III,5

The deep gully gives a tremendous winter adventure with a desperate section.
1) 3, 60m. Climb ice directly below the gully.
2) 2, 30m. Follow the snow slope to the gully.
3) 3, 25m. Gain the gully via a steep icy section, tough in lean conditions.
4) 1, 40m. Follow the snow gully to a cave.
5) 5, 45m. Exit the cave direct, or in lean conditions this can be skirted on the left.
6) 2, 120m. Romp up the upper gully.

Tremadog | Cwm Silyn | Cloggy | Llanberis | Lliwedd | Ogwen | Carneddau | Betws y Coed | Welsh Winter

❶ Gallipoli . . . ✩ 🖼 ☐ V,5
A fine and varied climb with good positions.
1) 4, 45m. Climb the icefall to a large snow-terrace and belay beneath a small roof.
2) 4, 45m. Traverse left and climb behind the detached pinnacle on the right of the shallow bay. Follow a groove above.
3) 5, 50m. Climb the narrow gully above, passing several steep and tricky sections.
4) 3, 50m. Continue up the gully.
5) 1, 50m. Easy snow remains.

❷ Passchendaele . . ✩ ☐ V,5
A brilliant winter adventure.
1) 5, 50m. Climb any of the steep turfy grooves to a ledge and a ramp leaning rightwards to gain the snow field.
2) 2, 60m. Climb easily across the snow field.
3) 3, 45m. Head up and right to steeper ground.
4) 4, 110m. Link the snow patches via a vague series of grooves, lots of options exist in this area.

❸ Flanders ✩ 🖼 🖼 ☐ VII,7
A tough and technical mixed route of great character. A must for any grade 7 leader. The original summer line can be followed at a slightly more technical but equally good VII,8.
1) 6, 35m. Start 10m left of *Western Gully*. Gain and climb a shallow groove to a small ledge on the edge of an arete. Continue up to a spike belay on a good ledge.
2) 7, 30m. Climb up and right to attack a groove on the right overlooking *Western Gully*.
3) 4, 55m. Traverse left and climb mixed icy ground to belay on a ledge.
4) 4, 55m. Trend left up more mixed icy ground to a good belay just left of a pinnacle.
5) 1, 30m. Scramble to the right side of the ridge to gain a chimney. Climb this chimney to gain a ledge. Belay beneath a groove.
6) 4, 30m. Follow the grassy groove to a small bay, step left to a corner and finish up a short crack in the final wall.
7) 1, 70m. Easily up the ridge to finish.

Flanders
The central buttress of the Black Ladders is now home to many complex mixed routes of a high standard. Shown here are some of the more classic lines and the neo-classic of *Flanders*.
Approach - All the routes start off the high terrace which can be approached by a variety of lines depending on conditions and ice build up.

Pinnacle

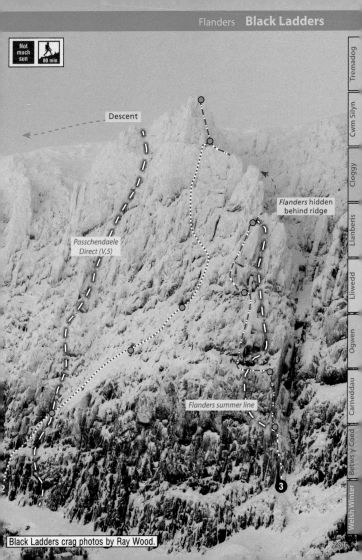

Not much sun

80 min

Descent

Flanders hidden behind ridge

Passchendaele Direct (V,5)

Flanders summer line

Black Ladders crag photos by Ray Wood.

Tremadog

Cwm Silyn

Cloggy

Llanberis

Lliwedd

Ogwen

Carneddau

Betws y Coed

Welsh Winter

Descent

Western Gully

The twisting precipice of *Western Gully* slices the right-hand side of the central buttress and gives an amazing adventure - especially when the direct finish is taken.

Approach - The route proper starts on the high terrace which can be approached directly up nice grade II ice in good conditions or from the right side in thin conditions.

❶ Western Gully 🕸 🖼 ☐ V,6

THE classic winter route of North Wales.

1) 3, 40m. Climb the gully, passing a narrow chimney-like section (peg) to a cave belay where the gully widens.

2) 4, 15m. Make an awkward move right around a jutting nose to gain a traverse line rightwards to a belay beneath a groove.

3) 5, 30m. Climb a thin technical pitch up a groove in the slab and traverse left to the large cave belay in the main gully.

4) 6, 12m. Step out right onto the thin and technical slab, and balance up this (1 or 2 pegs) to gain the gully above.

5) 4, 20m. Go up the gully and grapple round a steep chockstone boulder.

6) 1, 100m. Follow the easy gully to finish.

❷ Western Gully Direct Finish
🕸 🖼 ☐ V,5

This adds two excellent pitches of grade 5 ice heading up and right after the crux slab pitch of the original route.

1) 5, 25m. Climb a narrow icy gully on the right of the main gully to reach a small terrace and a tricky belay.

2) 5, 40m. Continue up the ice flow to reach easier ground and a good belay.

3) 2, 55m. An easy shallow gully leads to the summit.

Tremadog · Cwm Silyn · Cloggy · Llanberis · Llwedd · Ogwen · Carneddau · Betws y Coed · Welsh Winter

Icefall Gullies

On the right side of the Black Ladders is the scary classic *The Somme*, past this lies the two classics of *Icefall Gully Left* and *Right-hand*, and further to the right, on the highest section, the cliff offers many opportunities for adventure in icy and turfy features at around grade 3. Go and explore!

Not much sun | 80 min

Icefall Gully Right-hand (IV,4)

❸ The Somme ❄ V,6

A big route that tackles the left side of the impending black buttress.

1) 3, 45m. Climb the steep icy groove to a spike belay on the right at the large terrace.

2) 4, 15m. Make an awkward move rightwards around a jutting nose to gain a traverse line leftwards to a belay beneath a groove.

3) 5, 30m. Climb a thin technical pitch up a groove in the slab and traverse left to the large cave belay in the main gully.

4) 6, 30m. Step out right onto the thin and technical slab, and balance up this (1 or 2 pegs) to gain the gully above.

5) 4, 20m. Go up the gully and grapple round a steep chockstone boulder.

6) 1, 100m. Follow the easy gully to finish.

❹ Icefall Gully Left-hand
. . . . IV,4

Fantastic mid grade-ice climbing.

1) 2, 45m. Climb easy ice to a steepening.

2) 3, 45m. Follow more ice to a large ledge.

3) 4, 45m. Climb the steep left-hand icefall to gain a large ledge.

4) 3, 45m. Continue up a right facing groove to gain easy snowy ground.

5) 3, 45m. Climb easy snow then pass a steeper bulge-section to gain the upper gully.

6) 2, 120m. Aim up and left and follow steep snowy ground to the summit.

A good alternative to the previous route is the icy chimney 10m to the right which gives **Icefall Gully Right Hand, IV,4.**

Tremadog | Cwm Silyn | Cloggy | Llanberis | Lliwedd | Ogwen | Carneddau | Betws y Coed | Welsh Winter

Stars	Grade	Route	Photo	Page
**	E1	Agrippa		165
*	VS	Alpha		132
***	VDiff	Amphitheatre Buttress	161	161
*	Diff	Arete and Slab		131
*	Diff	Arete Climb		113
**	VDiff	Arete, The		147
***	E2	Aura		164
**	S	Avalanche/Red Wall/ Longland's Continuation	109	111
***	E4	Axe, The	57	64
**	E2	Barbarian		27
**	VS	Belle Vue Bastion		124
*	S	Bent		177
**	VS	Biceps Wall	155	159
**	E2	Black Cleft, The		67
*	VDiff	Black Gates, The		104
**	HVS	Black Spring		99
**	E2	Black Wall		77
*	VII	Blender Head		196
**	E3	Bloody Slab		70
**	HVS	Bochlwyd Eliminate		131
***	E4	Boldest, The		67
*	HS	Bombers Wall 1		172
*	Diff	Boo Boo Left-hand		46
*	HVS	Boot Crack		126
***	E1	Boulder, The		67
**	E2	Bovero		114
*	VS	Brant		83
***	HVS	Brant Direct		83
**	E2	Broadsword		167
*	VS	Brothers, The		41
*	HS	Bulging Wall		25
**	E3	Cadwaladr		167
**	E1	Canol		77
***	V	Cascade		183
**	V	Cascade Right-hand	180	183
***	III	Cave Gully		186
***	E1	Cemetery Gates	1	93
***	E1	Cenotaph Corner		93
**	III	Central Gully		199
***	VI	Central Icefall Direct		183
*	S	Central Rib		143
*	HS	Central Ridge		157
**	S	Central Route		151
**	III	Central Route		190
*	VS	Central Route 2		173
*	Diff	Central Slab Route		121
***	I/II	Central Trinity		185
**	VDiff	Charity		143
**	VDiff	Chasm Route		135
***	VI	Chequered Wall		183
*	VDiff	Chic		176
**	III	Chicane Gully		191
*	S	Chimney Climb		131
*	Mod	Chimney Crack		121
***	HS	Christmas Curry/Micah	33	34
***	E5	Cockblock		83
*	HVS	Continuation Crack		147
***	HVS	Corner, The		63
*	Mod	Crack 1		120
*	Diff	Crack 2		120
*	Diff	Crack 3		120
*	Diff	Crack 4		121
***	VS	Cracked Arete		158
***	IX	Cracking Up		196
***	HS	Cracks, The		97
***	S	Crackstone Rib		87
**	E3	Crazy Horse		126
**	HS	Creagh Dhu Wall		21
***	E4	Cream	25	39
**	E2	Crosscut		126
*	S	Crown of Thorns		77
***	E1	Crucible		51
**	IV	Curtain, The	178	193
**	VS	Curving Crack		60
*	E2	Daddy Cool		45
**	E3	Daurigol		59
**	E2	Death Wisher, The		114
**	E3	Demetreus		144
**	VI	Devil's Appendix, The	5	194
***	IV	Devil's Cellar, The		195
**	V	Devil's Filthbag, The		195
***	IV	Devil's Kitchen, The		193
***	III	Devil's Pasture	193	193
*	V	Devil's Pipes		191
***	V	Devil's Staircase		194
**	E1	Diadic		37
***	HVS	Diagonal Dinas Mot		97
*	HVS	Diagonal Route (Idwal)		147
*	HVS	Diglyph		131
*	VS	Direct Route (Dinas Mot)		97

Stars	Grade	Route	Photo	Page
*	VDiff	Direct Route (Milestone)		128
*	HS	Direct Route (Glyder Fach)		135
*	VS	Direct Route (Cyrau)		170
**	HVS	Direct Route, The (idwal)		143
***	HS	Dives/Better Things		91
*	S	Druid Route		133
**	III	Eastern Gully		199
***	VII	El Mancho		196
*	VS	Eliminate Start		170
**	E2	Erosion Groove Direct		89
*	E2	Excalibur		163
***	E2	Extraction		37
*	VDiff	Faith		144
***	E1	Falcon		29
*	VS	Fallen Block Crack		104
*	S	Falling Block Crack		22
***	HVS	Fang, The		37
**	E2	Ferdinand		114
***	E4	Fingerlicker		27
**	E2	First Amendment		83
*	E1	First Slip		42
*	S	Five Pitch Route		131
***	VII	Flanders		200
***	VDiff	Flying Buttress		91
***	VDiff	Fratricide Wall	168	174
*	V	Gallipoli		200
***	VDiff	Gambit Climb, The		103
*	S	Gamma		132
**	VDiff	Gashed Crag	116	123
*	E2	Gawain Direct		167
*	E3	Geireagle		45
**	HVS	Get Close		136
*	HVS	Gettysburg		163
***	E2	Grasper, The		32
***	HVS	Great Bow Combination		69
***	III	Great Gully		185
***	E4	Great Wall		60
*	IV	Grecian 2000		190
***	HVS	Grey Arete		141
***	VS	Grey Slab		141
*	VS	Grim Wall		41
**	E1	Grim Wall Direct		41
***	VS	Grimmett, The		163
**	S	Groove Above		147
***	VDiff	Grooved Arete		124
**	E1	Grooves, The		107
*	VS	Gwyndion		170
*	VS	Gwynedd		22
**	E4	Gwynhyfryd		167
**	VDiff	Hail Bebe		37
*	E2	Hand Traverse, The		65
***	E1	Hangover		85
***	VS	Hawks Nest Arete		136
*	S	Hawks Nest Buttress		136
*	E1	Hollow Men, The		136
*	VDiff	Hope		143
*	VDiff	Horned Crag Route		111
*	E2	Hywel Dda		173
*	IV	Icefall Gully Left-hand		203
***	E9	Indian Face, The		60
*	E1	Ivy Sepulchre		93
*	E2	Jabberwocky		51
***	HS	Jacob's Media		113
**	E1	Javelin Blade		147
*	VS	Javelin Buttress		147
***	E2	Jelly Roll		60
*	HS	Jingling Wall		172
*	HS	K.M.A		22
**	HVS	Kaisergebirge Wall		85
**	HVS	Karwendel Wall		85
*	HVS	Kirkus Direct (Ogof)		53
**	VS	Kirkus Route (Ogof)		53
**	S	Kirkus's Climb Direct (Oen)		176
***	VS	Kirkus's Route (Lloer)		156
*	VS	Knee Cap		159
**	III	Laddie's Gully		186
**	III	Ladies' Gully		186
***	VS	Lavaredo		174
***	HS	Lazarus		147
**	E1	Left Edge (Cloggy)		67
**	VDiff	Left Edge (Filliast)	148	151
***	E2	Left Wall	75	93
***	IV	Left-hand Branch		196
*	I/II	Left-hand Trinity		185
*	E1	Leg Slip		42
***	VS	Lightning Visit		174
*	VS	Lion		87
*	II/III	Little Gully		185
***	Diff	Little Tryfan Arete		120
***	E1	Llithrig		59
**	S	Long Climb Direct		173

Stars	Grade	Route	Photo	Page
**	VS	Longland's Climb		67
**	VS	Lorraine		97
***	HVS	Lot's Groove		135
**	VS	Lot's Wife		135
***	E3	Lubyanka		107
*	S	M.T.N.		23
**	VS	Madog		22
***	HS	Main Wall		107
**	HS	Marble Slab		131
**	E1	Meirionydd		25
**	HVS	Merlin Direct		45
***	HVS	Meshach		41
**	VS	Mistook		22
*	HVD	Mossy Slab		121
**	VS	Munich Climb		123
***	VS	Mur y Niwl		164
**	HVS	Myomancy		22
**	VS	Nea		81
*	E3	Neb Direct, The	18	34
***	E1	Nexus		101
**	VS	Nifl-Heim		42
*	E2	Nimbus		39
***	VS	Noah's Warning		91
*	Diff	North Arete		157
***	E3	November		60
*	S	Oberon		45
**	E1	Octo		64
**	E1	Old Holborn		89
***	VS	One Step in the Clouds		37
*	E1	One Step in the Crowds		21
*	Diff	Ordinary Route (Ogof)		53
*	Diff	Ordinary Route (Idwal)		143
***	VS	Original Route		147
*	E2	Orpheus		79
***	VDiff	Outside Edge Route		51
**	VDiff	Overlapping Ridge Route		123
**	E1	Overlapping Wall		87
***	VS	Oxine		114
*	HS	Paradise		111
**	Diff	Parson's Nose, The		103
***	V	Passchendaele		200
*	HVS	Pectoral Wall		159
*	HS	Pedestal Crack		63
*	E2	Pentangle		167
**	VS	Phantom Rib		81
**	VS	Pigott's Climb		59
***	V	Pillar Chimney		196
**	E2	Pincushion		27
**	E2	Pinnacle Arete		65
***	VDiff	Pinnacle Rib Route	2	123
**	VDiff	Pinnacle Ridge Route		149
***	S	Pinnacle Wall		163
***	E2	Pinnaclissima		163
*	VS	Piton Route		147
***	E1	Plexus		101
***	E1	Plum, The		34
*	E1	Plumbagin		164
**	E5	Poacher, The		114
**	S	Poor Man's Peuterey		26
*	E2	Pretzl Logic		42
**	E3	Private Practice		172
*	VS	Pryderi		170
***	E6	Psych'n'Burn	28	29
**	VDiff	Pulpit Route		128
**	V	Pyramid Face Direct		199
*	IV	Pyramid Gully		199
***	E3	Quasar		85
**	VS	Quatre Fois Direct		25
*	VS	Rammer's Route		22
***	III	Ramp, The		193
*	E1	Rampart Corner		147
**	VDiff	Rectory Chimneys		104
***	E4	Resurrection		93
**	VDiff	Rib and Slab		77
*	S	Rib, The		156
**	VS	Ribstone Crack		89
**	VS	Rift Wall		79
***	E5	Right Wall		93
**	III	Right-hand Branch		197
**	II/III	Right-hand Trinity		186
*	VS	Ring, The		103
*	Diff	Route I		133
**	Diff	Route II		133
*	HVS	Route of Knobs		104
*	Diff	Rowan Route		128
**	E2	Rowan Tree Slabs		144
***	VS	Sabre Cut		91
**	VS	Scimitar Crack		138
*	E2	Scorpio		63
**	VS	Scratch		27
***	HVS	Scratch Arete		27

Stars	Grade	Route	Photo	Page
***	IV	Screen, The	178	193
***	VS	Shadow Wall		89
**	VS	Shadrach	3	41
**	VS	Sheaf		69
***	E2	Shrike		64
**	HVS	Sickle		83
***	E2	Silhoutte		63
***	E3	Silly Arete		27
*	HS	Skylon		87
*	VDiff	Slab 1		120
*	S	Slab 2		120
**	VDiff	Slab Climb		135
*	HS	Slab Climb Right-hand		71
**	S	Slack		177
*	S	Slanting Chimney		71
**	E2	Slape Direct		83
**	VS	Slow Ledge Climb		98
**	HS	Soapgut		126
***	V	Somme, The		203
***	IV	South Gully		190
***	HVS	Spectre		81
**	E2	Spectrum		81
*	E2	Spiral Scratch		163
***	VDiff	Spiral Stairs		91
**	E2	SS Special		83
*	Diff	Stepped Crack		121
**	V	Sting, The		195
***	HVS	Strapiombo		26
**	VS	Striptease		37
***	E3	Stroll On		85
***	VDiff	Sub Cneifion Rib	119	138
*	E1	Subsidiary Grooves		107
*	Mod	Subsidiary Slab		113
*	VS	Sunset Crack		59
***	HVS	Super Direct (Milestone)	95	128
***	E1	Super Direct (Dinas Mot)		97
*	VS	Sword/Route 2, The		112
*	E2	Temper		159
**	E2	Ten Degrees North		101
***	HS	Tennis Shoe		143
**	E1	Terminator		112
**	VIII	Travesty		196
**	III	Trinity Buttress		186
***	E2	Troach, The		63
*	S	Two Pitch Route		131
*	VDiff	Underlap		151
*	HVS	Unicorn		87
*	Diff	Upper Staircase, The		147
**	HS	Valerie's Rib		32
***	E2	Vector		39
***	E1	Vember		60
*	E3	Venom		42
***	E3	Void		39
***	E3	Vulcan		29
***	E4	Vulture		45
*	HS	Wall Climb		131
*	E2	Wasp, The		21
*	Mod	Waved Slab		151
***	E2	Weaver, The		39
***	E3	West Buttress Eliminate		69
**	HVS	West Rib		98
*	V	Western Gully		202
***	V	Western Gully Direct Finish		202
**	VS	Western Slabs		98
***	E2	White Slab		69
**	HVS	Wind	72	85
*	E2	Wrack, The		131
**	VDiff	Wrinkle, The		87
***	E5	Wrinkled Retainer		126
*	HVS	Y Broga		45
*	HVS	Yellow Crack		89
**	VS	Yellow Groove		79
**	E2	Yellow Wall		79
*	VS	Yogi		47
*	VS	Zig Zag		77
**	VS	Zip Groove		158
*	HS	Zip Wall		158

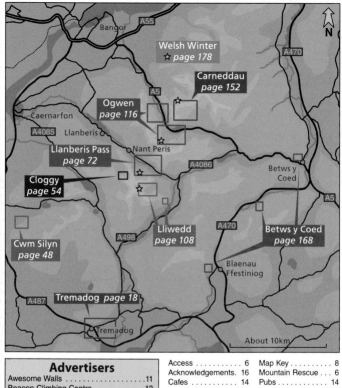

Map showing locations:

- Bangor — A55
- Welsh Winter ☆ *page 178*
- Carneddau *page 152*
- Ogwen *page 116*
- Caernarfon
- A4085 — Llanberis
- Llanberis Pass *page 72*
- Nant Peris
- A4086
- Betws y Coed
- Cloggy *page 54*
- Cwm Silyn *page 48*
- A498
- Lliwedd *page 108*
- A470
- Betws y Coed *page 168*
- Blaenau Ffestiniog
- Tremadog *page 18*
- A487
- Tremadog
- A5
- A470

About 10km

N

Access 6
Acknowledgements. 16
Cafes 14
Classic Routes 12
Clothing 10
Colour Codes 12
Gear 10
Grade Table 12
Guidebooks 6
Guides 14
Introduction. 2

Map Key 8
Mountain Rescue . . . 6
Pubs 14
Ropes 10
Route Index 204
Shops 14
Symbol Key. 8
Topo Key. 8
Walls 14
Winter Introduction . . 4
Winter Grades 4

Mountain Rescue
Dial 999 and ask for 'POLICE - MOUNTAIN RESCUE'